The Being of God

THE
BEING OF GOD

*Theology and the
Experience of Truth*

Robert P. Scharlemann

THE SEABURY PRESS / NEW YORK

1981
The Seabury Press
815 Second Avenue
New York, N.Y. 10017

Library of Congress Cataloging in Publication Data

Scharlemann, Robert P
   The being of God.

   Bibliography: p. 190
   Include index.
   1. Truth. 2. God. I. Title.
BT50.S372   231'.042   80-25281
ISBN 0-8164-0494-1

Contents

Preface

Once done, a work should be able to stand on its own without an elaborate explanation of what it is and how it came to be. But a book written on the experience of truth may call for a brief explanatory preface; for the combination of experience and truth is somewhat odd in itself, and to include theology in it may compound the puzzle, since theology is still most often thought of as a matter of proclamation or confession but not of verification, the reasons for which I have indicated in the first chapter. No one today would seriously contend that truth in religion, truth in art, and truth in science and the humanities are ascertained in exactly the same way; but how they are ascertained, and what the connection is among them, remain problematic. The debate about the nature of truth is, moreover, not an academic matter alone; for an interest in truth constitutes an essential characteristic of human beings as such. It can be disguised, it can be made light of or subordinated to other interests. But, underneath, the interest in truth remains one of the essential motives of human existence. This very circumstance would justify the continuing efforts to find—if one may put it so—the truth about truth. But, in addition, there is a particular aspect that, as suggested by the title of the book, is worthy of attention because it has been neglected or overlooked—truth is, in its own way, a matter of experience. What that way is and how truth is connected to other objects of experience are central concerns of the present study. It would not be exaggerating to say that, without the experience of truth, no sanity in the rest of experience would be possible at all. Accordingly, I have directed attention away from theories about the nature of truth in order to show how truth enters experience. Besides putting the emphasis where, as it seems to me, it belongs, this shift also makes it possible to start from a basis that does not need to appeal to any particular philosophical or theological school for justification and to allow the theme to unfold on its own terms for anyone who may care to follow it.

By this, I do not mean that no philosophical and theological positions are involved. Obviously, the opposite is the case. But I do mean that no particular "school" authority or idiom is invoked. I have drawn on materials, philosophically speaking, from both the Anglo-American analytical and the Continental phenomenological and speculative traditions; but the choice of materials was determined not by a school-bridging aim but by what seemed most directly pertinent and illuminating. Of course, this can be done only if an author is willing to answer both philosophically and theologically for the positions that are taken. And that is part of the intention. For purposes of a preface, the following observations may serve to set the stage.

The question of how truth is experienced, and what might even be meant by an "experience" of truth, remains basic. The answer that this study develops, however, can be sketched briefly so as to provide an initial orientation for the reader. First, I identify experience, in distinction from mere thought or unintelligible sensation, as involving something that is *given to* thought. This formulation obviously has Kantian roots, but its sense is well anchored in English usage, and it could be supported by a systematics of reflection. Such a systematics, however, is not undertaken here; it may be at most noticeable in certain allusions made in the course of the chapters.

Second, the experience of truth is understood as that of seeing a certain kind of "identity in difference," a formulation referring to two basic laws of thought, which appear in tautologies and contradictions respectively. The significance of these laws is not often the subject of attention today, but it preoccupied post-Kantian speculative idealists, one of whom (Karl Daub) I have thought worth recovering for discussion here. In this case too, however, the use of materials from speculative idealism does not serve the purpose of providing a school sanction to what is said. Instead, its main purpose is to provide material for illuminating the line of thought that is being drawn, and its secondary purpose is the historical one of making known a phase of intellectual history that is unfamiliar.

Third, while the act of seeing identity in difference is an experience because it involves something given to the mind, still its object is not direct but "reflective" or, as it may also be called, "intentional"; that is to say, the matter which is seen as identity in difference is not a physical object—obviously—but is given in or "upon" the physical object. It involves a reality—a structure relating the meaning which is understood to the physical appearance which is perceived—that is a datum. Experience that has to do with such reflective objects is here called "reflective" experience and is distinguished from the "direct" experience of physical objects. There is no generally accepted terminology to designate these two different orders of experience and their corresponding objects, and the terms may not be the best-chosen. But what is meant should in any case be clear—direct experience involves objects that can be given to the mind through the physical senses (trees, stones, etc.), and reflective experience involves second-order objects, such as truth, that are given in and through those objects. These matters are discussed at greater length below. Here I want only to call attention to them. When we see the truth of a statement, we are indeed seeing something that is there, but we can see it only through a comparison of the meaning of a statement with the real appearance of the object or state of affairs to which it refers. In other words, reflection is not only a nonexperiential recalling or contemplation of experience; it can also involve an experience of its own, and it is the only way of experiencing the distinctness of such second-order objects as "truth." If a label is to be placed upon this view, it might be that of a "new realism."

Fourth, in what seems to me potentially the most fruitful (and perhaps also problematic) aspect of the theme, I have brought the positive-scientific and the reflective-humanistic sides of truth together in the conception that identity in difference means either the identity of substance in a difference in time (the substance and time of what is said and of what is so) or the identity of time in a difference in subjects (the time and subject in what is said and in what occurs). No discussion of time can avoid Martin Heidegger, and I have not attempted to do so; but I have concentrated on his treatment of verification and of the onto-theological character of Western metaphysics. To it I have added a more extensive discussion with Hans-Georg Gadamer's hermeneutics, which seems to me to offer more for understanding the experience of truth than either Gadamer himself or his expositors and critics have heretofore made explicit.

The philosophic work that may have been the most influential for the systematic frame of the whole is noted only in the bibliography—Hans Wagner's *Philosophie und Reflexion*. It does not appear in the body of the work chiefly because its influence is to be found not so much in particular material as in its mediation of a philosophic tradition.

Finally, in a treatise of this nature one cannot ignore the question of the point of view from which the observations are made and the standpoint that is taken. Both these topics are explicitly treated below. Here it is sufficient, by way of anticipation, to say that the point of view initially adopted is not theological but that of reflection itself, until the inner problematics of this position call it into question.

The preceding philosophical considerations will not obscure the theological interest of this study. Since the concern is with truth in theology, the bulk of material comes from the theological tradition, though selectively and, necessarily, somewhat arbitrarily. In incorporating this tradition, I have reworked some materials that are very familiar (such as the "five ways" of Thomas Aquinas), some not so familiar (like Karl Barth's analysis of Anselm's theological principle), and some virtually unknown (such as Daub's essay on the logic of the divine names). Again, equally selectively and somewhat arbitrarily, I have joined discussion with only a few current authors—some, like Ebeling and Altizer, better known than others. This is admittedly limited, but it seems warranted by an interest in keeping the whole from becoming unmanageable. The final section, regarding the verificational importance of Paul Tillich's interpretation of the symbol of the cross, will perhaps signify that it is his theology, more than any other, which incorporates this decisive insight.

About the genesis of this book only a few words need to be added. It was more than a generation ago that the question of truth was raised, particularly through the efforts of analytical philosophers, in the form of the verification of assertions, and the resulting debate was incorporated in differing ways into theology as well. The course of the discussion has been charted several times already, recently by Patrick Sherry in *Religion, Truth and Language Games*, and need not be repeated here. But its harvest, as Sherry observed, has been small and disappointing for religious thought. Why so, and is there a way around it? This was one of the questions that started the research and thought leading to this book. Two other major factors, however, entered into its shaping over a period of years. One was a continuing conversation about the relations between contemporary science and theology, especially in matters methodological, that formed the content of some courses and seminars I have given over the past decade together with William Klink, a physicist at this University. The other was a year spent, under the auspices of a Fulbright-Hays grant, in research on the work of Karl Daub, a nearly forgotten but, in his time, major representative of the speculative idealism that, in the wake of Kant's critique, sought to reconstruct, or at least to refound, the edifice of Christian theology in view of the criticism. It was in connection with this research, if not a direct result of it, that the pattern which has now been set forth finally began to come into view, though it is a pattern that, one suspects, would be initially as alien to speculative idealism as to critique and to positivism. Another three years, and more revisions than one would care to remember, were needed before the whole could be worked out in a moderately satisfactory way; but the result is presented herewith.

Robert P. Scharlemann
Iowa City
June 1980

1

The Experience of Truth as a Theological Problem

Si enim ibi [sc. in beatissima Trinitate] est summa communicatio et vera diffusio, vera est ibi origo et vera distinctio.
—Bonaventure, *Itinerarium*, 6,3

Religion, through its holiness, and law, through its majesty, commonly try to exempt themselves [from critique].
—Kant, *Critique of Pure Reason*, A xii

The origin and the epitome of all truth is this that God is not hidden, but open, to himself.
—Karl Barth, *KD*, I/1, p. 73

Truth plays a split role in theological thinking and theological science. It is asserted, but it always seems to run headlong into insuperable barriers when the question is asked how this truth is ascertained or experienced. That theology asserts truth, but does not show how this truth can be experienced, is doubtless one of the reasons for the perpetual uneasiness that its assertions seem to arouse. They have to do with matters that should be of importance, and yet what real bearing they have on the other, daily matters of importance is difficult to see. Without such a connection theology is reduced to the officially espoused position of a religious body—or to the beliefs held by a religious group, whose importance is then derived from the political or social significance of the group otherwise; or it is promulgated by thoughtless speech and empty words.

This problem is not new, of course; but it seems to become

1

urgent at times like the present when the mind's devotion is being solicited from all sides by ideologies and promises beyond counting. The common sense of which the Anglo-Saxon heritage prides itself provides a certain standard by which to measure them. But common sense can break down; indeed, it has already been broken down by the time one begins to think about such questions as the nature of truth. In such circumstances it affords no guidelines for evaluating the simultaneous appeal and impertinence of matters theological.

In the present book an effort is made to show how the true or, as the case may be, the false can be experienced in theological assertions. To couple experience and truth breaks with a pattern fixed by Kantian philosophy, in which experience is always directed to objects that can be exhibited or presented to the physical senses. Truth, obviously, is not a physical object. To speak of the possibility of experiencing it is, therefore, to make use of a division different from the Kantian. Though the Kantian division is taken as virtually self-evident in most contemporary science, with the possible exception of quantum physics, there is a good reason for not adopting it: it is simply inadequate. Above all, the division of everything into objects of experience, which are physically perceptible, on one side, and the pure forms of thought on the other, with a nod in between to the transcendental objectivity that is constituted by the forms of time and space, leaves out of account the whole realm of reflective objects to which truth belongs. Such things as truth are neither physical objects nor pure forms of thought, nor are they transcendental conditions of experience; for they are objects that appear, although that to which they appear is reflection instead of physical sensations.

There is a purpose to insisting initially that truth is not merely a thought form nor a meaning but an object. The justification for this contention can come later, but the purpose of the initial insistence is to steer the line of thought away from the possibility, which might otherwise seem attractive, that theology has to do with meaning but not with truth and that what is important

about theological assertions is their power to present meanings
to contemplate instead of their truthful, or untruthful, connection to something that is other than thinking and language;
namely, to that which is called "being." Such a view, as espoused,
for example, in *The Life of the Mind* by Hannah Arendt, has a
point, of course; for the objects to which the mind in its capacity
as reason—*Vernunft* rather than *Verstand*—is related are not
physically perceptible as are trees and stones, nor are they
hypotheses about or interpretations of physical objects; they are,
rather, meanings directly present to mind and worth thinking
about. They empower mind by giving it something to think
about, and in that sense they constitute the life of mind. To
identify them, however, by saying that reason is concerned with
meaning but not with being, or reality, is to confuse the distinction between meaning, as the sense carried by signs, and reflective objects, as those realities which are *given* to the mind even
though they are not physically perceptible.

To lay the foundation for a discussion of truth in theology, it is
advisable first to delimit what is meant by the experience of truth
as such, that is, the structure that is implicit in all particular
expressions of this experience. It is not the concern here to
elaborate a theory about truth, though as the discussion proceeds some account must be taken of the several different
theories; rather, it is to provide a description of an experience,
called the experience of truth, and to provide it so that we are
clear on what is being talked about and so that we have some way
of seeing whether what is said about that experience is so. The
description is intended, therefore, to be a true account of the
experience of truth.

The Phenomenon of Truth

The conception that reflection is not merely an addendum to
daily, literal experience but also involved in it as a second level of
that experience, and that we can speak accordingly not only of
reflection but also of reflective *experience*, introduces a useful
possibility for description and analysis—that objects can be given

as real even though they are not presented by way of sensation. The tree that is a physical object and that can be perceived through the senses is a reality; seeing it as such is an experience of that physical object. The sense understood in an assertion (as when one reads or hears "This is a tree" and knows what those words say although one does not see what "this" is pointing out) is a meaning. Truth as it is experienced is neither a meaning nor a sensational object but something reflectively experienced when one "sees" how a meaning and a datum correspond to each other by pointing to each other and filling out each other. It is, therefore, proper to speak of "seeing" or "hearing" the truth, for the application of these terms to such an object is a matter not of metaphorical usage but of the reflective aspect of the literal meaning of the words. Reflective experience and sense experience can make use of the same vocabulary because they are intertwined as the first and the other aspect of the whole experience. Which is regarded as the first, and which the other, does not matter; what matters is that the two coinhere.

Against this background, what is meant by the "experience of truth" can be stated thus: *To experience truth is to see the identity in the difference between meaning and reality.* A statement about something (for example, "The leaf is green") is different from the thing itself (the green leaf), but what it says is "the same as" what is so; and seeing this same in the different is the experience of truth. It is clear that truth, as such a reflective object, can be distinguished from objects of sensation only when a distinction can be made between understanding the sense of words and perceiving the reality to which they refer. If we could not distinguish between the two (difference), and if we could not see that how we think of something is the same as how that thing shows itself to be (identity), we could not experience truth as such. Truth is given to experience not through sensation or thought alone but through an act in which a meaning understood is compared with a datum perceived.

Theological expressions, however, seem to present a special problem, for there seems to be no way of perceiving their referent so as to compare what it is with what is said about it. Anything that appears is less than God. There is no standpoint outside of everything from which to see and to judge whether what is said of God is true. At least this is the case if the God we have in mind is one than whom no greater can be thought. How, for example, would it be possible to see whether the assertion "God was in Christ reconciling the world" agrees with what is so? Since on the face of the matter it seems to be impossible, if not perverse, to see whether this is true, a long tradition contends that truth in theological assertions cannot be experienced but only believed or credited on authority or confessed. This tradition is still effective partly because how we see all things is in large measure a matter of tradition, and we do not often distinguish between seeing them and seeing truth in them, but partly also because the protagonist of the opposite position, metaphysical thought, has been seriously crippled, if not mortally wounded. Western metaphysics, under the motto of *sapere aude*—dare to know and not merely to opine—stands on the premise that seeing the necessity or impossibility of thought itself is nothing else than the experience of eternal truth or falsehood.

Metaphysical thinking of this sort has a similarity to common experience of objects. When we have an object (such as a green leaf) before us in clear view, we are not free to think that it is other than what it is. Our thought is constrained by how the object presents itself; we cannot connect sensation and thought according to will but must do so according to how the thing permits itself to be perceived. To think "This is a tiger" when we are in actual view of a leaf does violence to the experience and destroys the thought of that object. We *must* think of it as a leaf if we are to think of it as it really is. This constraint upon thought, which prevents us from thinking as we will in certain circumstances, is the mark of "experience"—something is *given to* thought. In this sense being, as it presents itself in physical objects, represents necessity and not freedom for thinking. This common experiential fact is expanded metaphysically to objects beyond sense experience according to the rule that what must be thought to be so, and cannot be thought otherwise, must be so. In this case, however, necessity is imposed upon thought not by how what is so presents itself in an object but by the intrinsic law of thinking itself. "We cannot think otherwise" then signifies not that thinking is constrained by the appearance of an object, but that the opposite thought is self-contradictory. This produces what Kant called the dialectical illusion of the ideas of pure reason—that the necessity of thinking, as imposed by its own rules of correct formation, substitutes for the self-presentation of an object. In so doing, necessity of thought serves as an intellectual intuition, the envisagement of nonsensible appearances, and replaces the sense perception that is part of common experience. The effect of this substitution in theology is illustrated in the discussion of the being of God by the way that Bonaventure, for example, appeals to "being" and "goodness" as the names of God from which we gain knowledge of him. If "God" is a designation of primary being, then, Bonaventure infers, "it is *impossible to think* of him as not being" (*Itinerarium*, 5,6; emphasis added); and since what is simply best is "that than which nothing better can be thought," this best "cannot rightly be thought not to be, since to be is at any rate (*omnino*) better than not to be" (6,2).[1]

This metaphysical application of the necessity of thought was undermined by the philosophy that begins with Kant's critiques of reason, for criticism made clear the radical difference between the constraint imposed on thinking by how a real thing actually presents itself to the senses and the necessity of thought which is that of the logical rules themselves.[2] Deducing the existence of a transcendent world beyond experience makes use of one necessity (that of clear and correct thinking) as though it were the other necessity (that imposed by how objects present themselves). This dialectical illusion can be exposed, however, by a feature of thinking itself; namely, that it is not necessary to think that the necessity of thought is a reflection of reality. Metaphysical thinking (in this sense of metaphysics) is thus undermined from within.

But if metaphysics is no longer in a position to determine the truth of theological assertions, the possibility of experiencing truth in theology seems to be lost. The question "Is it true that some trees have green leaves?" can be answered by seeing whether what we understand as "trees having green leaves" corresponds with what we can perceive when we look at trees. Similarly, whether the sixteenth president of the United States bore the name of Lincoln can be determined—to state a complex procedure simplistically—by looking at lists of presidents and at a history of the country. Finally, whether Jesus was resurrected after being put to death can be determined by whether the person called Jesus was at one time dead and at some later time showed himself as recognizably the same person living in a transformed body. (If the body were not transformed, the man would have been resuscitated but not resurrected.) Perhaps our records of that time are not sufficient to determine the answer with a very high degree of assurance. But in principle one can determine whether the assertion is true by seeing whether what the words mean is the same as what is or was so.

None of these questions, not even that of the resurrection of Jesus, is directed to a theological assertion. The matter is different, however, when it is asked whether God raised (or did not raise) Jesus from the dead and whether *God* chose Lincoln as the sixteenth president. In these cases it seems to be impossible to see for ourselves whether what is said agrees with what is so. Did God make the universe? A wag may answer, "If God didn't, no one did." A biblicist may answer, "Consult the Bible. It says he did." But even a biblicist cannot see whether what the Bible says is the same as what is so. The truth or untruth of theological assertions seems to lie beyond all possible experience.

Barth put the problem precisely. "Only God *himself* can speak of God," he wrote in "Das Wort Gottes als Aufgabe der Theologie" (1922); we are human beings and as such we cannot speak of God. It is no escape from this impossibility to say that the name "Jesus Christ" is, for Christian theology, a word that not only might be but is God's speaking himself. For which of us,

Barth asked, is in a position to say not merely "It could be so" but "It is so"? Barth concluded that we can deal with this dilemma only by recognizing both the impossibility and the necessity of speaking of God and, in so doing, give God the glory. Theological assertions are rightly expected to be not human words but words of God; yet they are always words of human beings. This dividedness between the legitimate expectation that theology be what its name suggests and the just recognition that it cannot be that—in other words, the recognition that, by default, theological assertions are always false—constitutes the peculiar jeopardy, or, as Barth called it, the *Bedrängnis*, of theology in the matter of truth. In retrospect it seems clear that Barth, who saw the problem so clearly in the 1920s, found no solution to it, other than for the theologian to speak as though his saying were God's saying—this is the notion of witness or confession—and to see what happens. It may happen that the human words become the word of God. But nothing is more useless than to try to find in Barth's theology an indication of how one can tell whether the word of God has actually happened. The "proclaimed word of God" means, in its most intimate sense, "human speech of God in which and through which God himself speaks of himself" (*KD*, I/1, p. 97), speech which is true according to God's own judgment. We, however, do not have that judgment in hand (I/1, p. 95). Thus Barth of the *Church Dogmatics*.

The difficulty may prompt the charge that the very effort to seek an experience of truth in theology is perverse. Indeed, religion—by which I mean any consciousness, or the consciousness in any person, for which "God" and related words name a realm that is as real as the physical world because the images created by those words are as much givens as are the data of sense perception—may find itself imperiled by it. The religious mentality—a mentality already lost by the time one speaks about it as such—seems instinctively to recognize that as soon as one questions whether what presents itself as divine is really divine, the game is, as it were, over and lost. The very raising of the question makes an appeal to something more basic than the apparent divinity itself and thereby denies the godliness of the appearance. Questioning the godliness of the apparent God in the interest of truth opens a dimension of being that we can designate only by such terms as "fall," a precipitous movement from a place to which there is no return. It puts the religious consciousness into the irrevocable past. Religion can never experience truth as such or as distinct from the object upon which truth appears. It is in the strange position of being able to experience truth only so long as it does not know about or ask about it as truth. That theology, qua theology and not as critique, is often reluctant to accept the task of formulating the question of its own truth reflects a remembrance of this religious relation. It is worth calling attention to this rooting, for doing so indicates that the anxiety often awakened by theological questions is not merely a psychological phenomenon but a consequence of the character of the original religious relation as such. Theology, while it is not religion, can be affected by religion so as to become religious thought, a thinking that is an unreflective "thanking" in the presence of an appearing deity. In the *Church Dogmatics* Barth's conception of theology has this quality. Christian theology, he writes, moves in a circle designated by two answers to the question "Who is God?" The first answer is that the Revealer (that is, the Trinitarian God) is God; the second is that "this, *our* God" is God. "Christian theology can mean nothing else than an exercise in this movement" (*KD*, I/1, 401).

More particularly, what disrupts the religious relation is the critical question of whether appearance is reality. Had Abraham, for example, asked whether the command to sacrifice his son was really a command of Elohim, he could not have suspended the ethical in his obedience to its unconditional power. In post-Kantian thought critique has been shaped by Feuerbach and Freud, who fashioned the prospect that the deity is nothing other than a dissembled human consciousness. "In the object of religion which we call *theos* in Greek and *Gott* in German, nothing but the essence of man is expressed," Feuerbach declared at the beginning of the third lecture he delivered on the topic "The

Essence of Religion" at Heidelberg in 1848 (*WR*, p. 10). "God is the nature of man regarded as absolute truth" (*Essence*, p. 19). What religion is aware of in the image of God, with his attributes and deeds, is indeed a truth about something, Feuerbach granted. But it is truth in an illusory form; for what relgion is about is not really God but human being generically; the opposition that religion makes between God and human being is, when uncovered, a contrast between the species *homo* and the individual member of the species. "Religion, at least the Christian, is the relation of man to . . . his own nature . . . viewed as a nature apart from his own" (*Essence*, p. 14).

Feuerbach's view, repeated more pessimistically by Freud, is, nonetheless, not so radical a challenge as that which ultimately is implied in the Hegelian system of the absolute, the *Science of Logic*. With respect to Feuerbach, we can at least still think of alternate possibilities—either the deity is the subject it appears in religion to be, or it is an image for human nature. Both of them permit a hermeneutic of trust as well as a hermeneutic of suspicion. But with respect to the absoluteness of the principles of thinking, the barrier is erected by our not even being able to think of a second possibility. All conceivable alternatives have already been overtaken by the absoluteness of the thinking process itself. We cannot, as it seems, even put the question of whether God is a subject other than, or outside of, the edifice of absolute thinking. To say that God is not the absolute is as much a part of absolute thought as is saying that God is the absolute. The absoluteness of thought has no exit. Nietzsche later saw that the only relief from this absolute deity is the cataclysmic event of the death of this God. Dialectical theology, taking its cue from Kierkegaard, sought to escape from the impasse by speaking of God as wholly other, *totaliter aliter*, in order to distinguish between absoluteness and Godhood. But to do so only relocates the question. The *totaliter alius* may be nothing, and dialectical theology may thus be unmasked as nihilism in disguise. If so, dialectical theology turns out to be but a dissimulation of nihilist ideology. Far from escaping the critique of religion, it falls victim to it.

Raising such questions within theology seems to attack the very foundations. If *we* are to judge whether the word "God" arises from deception, whether God is other than the absolute, and whether there is a difference between "wholly other" and "nothing," then the position from which we must make the judgment is from the very start assumed to be superior to the God being judged. But then God is not God, and the effort to see the truth of theological assertions inevitably fails.

In the preceding paragraphs the experience of truth was described by reference to assertions. But the identity in difference that characterizes truth can appear in other ways. Friends can be "true"; there can be "true" statesmen; and people can be "true" to their word. In common usage and in the history of thought truth has three senses: first, the correspondence between what is thought (or said) and what is really so; second, the manifestation of being in what is there; and, third, the constancy of being. Truth, which appears when true assertions are made, may make its appearance in these other forms as well and is recognizable as the same phenomenon because it exhibits the same structure of identity in difference.

Commonly and most directly truth is taken to involve a correspondence or agreement between what is said and what is so.[3] To experience it is to see that correspondence. This is the conception described above. It is expressed in the Aristotelian definition that has come to us from Isaac ben Israeli's *Book of Definitions: veritas est adequatio (convenientia, correspondentia) intellectus et rei*, truth is the adequation (coming together, correspondence) of understanding and reality. As Aquinas formulates it in *Contra Gentiles*, "truth of understanding (*intellectus*) is the suitability (*adaequatio*) of understanding and reality according to which the understanding says that what is is and what is not is not" (1,59). Not only particular assertions but also mental pictures of the whole of reality can be so understood. Truth in theology then has to do with whether a picture of the whole of things that contains the universe and God is more in agreement with how things really are than one that contains only the universe. No prescription concerning how to ascertain such a correspondence is contained in this conception as such. With some kinds of statements the correspondence may be determined empirically ("the leaf is green"); with others, experientially ("skating is fun"); and with still others, experimentally ("the force of a falling body is equivalent to mass multiplied by acceleration"). But in all of them truth appears as a correspondence, or agreement, between what is said and what is so, between *intellectus* and *res*.

Although this sense of truth may be the most common, it is not the only one to be found in the use of the word. Truth is experienced not only upon assertions but also upon things, persons, and even words. That someone is a true friend is an example. The truth of the statement that N is a friend is, of course, different from the truth of N's friendship; but both are appearances of truth. If the truth of statements lies in their agreement with what is so, the truth of N's friendship has to do with whether what N is agrees with the idea of what a friend ought to be. This is what Hegel called the deeper sense of truth—the agreement between reality and the idea. What something is may correspond to what, according to our idea, it ought to be. N lives up to the idea of a friend and thus shows himself as a true friend. In such a case too it is truth that appears and is experienced reflectively.

There is an additional element. What we experience as truth in a true friend is also the constancy of the friendship. A true friend is one who remains such even when circumstances change; a false friend is one who in some circumstances appears to be (and perhaps is) a friend but who, in other circumstances, shows himself not to be one. Similarly, although being true to one's word does mean binding oneself in such a way that one's behavior corresponds with what one has promised, it also means that the self-obligation is not restricted to the moment when the promise is given, but endures until it is fulfilled in the deed to which it points.

Such assertions as "N is a true statesman" and "N is a true friend" may be interpreted according to either or both forms of truth. They may be understood to say that what N is agrees with the idea of what a statesman and a friend should be; N fits the ideal. Or they may be understood to say something about the constancy with which the person is a statesman or a friend. Or they may mean both. But to experience truth in them is to see the identity in difference that is either the agreement of the entity with the idea or the endurance of the same through different times and circumstances.

A third sense of truth is indicated by the etymology of the Greek word for truth. *Aletheia*—as Heidegger's *Being and Time* and *The Essence of Truth* brought to general attention earlier this century—is truth in the sense of coming to light; the truth of something is its having been, or its being, brought out of a state in which it is not noticed or remembered into a state of notice and recall. That this is not an esoteric or especially mysterious event, as detractors of Heidegger would have one believe, can be shown by an example. Imagine a desk cluttered with paper, books, clips, and a host of other things. Looking at the desk we register nothing but a confused image. At that moment someone says, "There is a pencil on the desk," and this statement brings to light, or makes us see, an object which, in our confused gaze, we had not even noticed. In doing so, it shows its power to detect an object that had been previously hidden. A statement that thus lifts an entity out of an undifferentiated background is true in the sense of *aletheuein*—it clears, it reveals, it lets something stand out against this background. Every bilingual or multilingual person knows of this occurrence. A text or a speech which is clear in its original language becomes obscure when translated into another because the words of the second language do not let the subject matter stand out as do those of the original. So too, when Schleiermacher (*CF*, §11, p. 54) speaks of the redemption-liberation (*Erlösung*) accomplished by Jesus as a passing and deliverance from a state of God-forgetfulness to one of God-consciousness, the truth experienced upon the figure of Jesus has the sense of *aletheia*, the revealing of God to a consciousness that had not noticed deity at all.

The sense of truth as manifestation may not be the usual one. Yet it is an ingredient in the phenomenon as experienced. To "speak the truth" means to speak not merely so that the statements made correspond with what is so, but also so that what is hidden or forgotten or unnoticed is brought to light. The truth of such aphorisms as E.E. Cummings's "Equality is what does not exist among equals" ("Jottings," p. 70) lies not primarily in a correspondence between meaning and reality but in their ability to uncover a matter by making us think. To "speak the truth" is, as Schleiermacher's term "God-forgetfulness" and Heidegger's term "forgetfulness of being" suggest, to awaken the hearer from an amnestic state in which what is there is not seen or noticed.

Aletheia is the other face of identity in difference: to experience it is to experience the difference in an identity. Greek philosophy reflected the emergence of difference out of the identical—the difference, for example, between words and things (Gadamer, *TM*, p. 378). Modern usage reflects the opposite aspect—the discovery of the identical in the different, a direction already indicated in Aristotle's relating of experience to memory (*Met.*, 980b28) since memory and "unforgotten" are obviously connected. But the whole truth involves both. Thus, the assertion "There is a pencil on the desk" can be true to the extent that it differentiates something against an undifferentiated background which is still in mind, for then the difference exists in the identity—the pencil stands out against the cluttered desk top. If either the identity of the background or the differentiation is eliminated, truth cannot be experienced. *Aletheia* presupposes identity, as correspondence presupposes difference.

From Anselm to Schleiermacher in the Christian tradition the experience of truth upon the word and idea "God" was made possible by the difference and the identity between the supreme being of metaphysics and the biblical God. As long as the difference between the God of the Bible and the being of Greek ontology was not forgotten, metaphysical theology provided a second movement in which the one as God and the one as being were identified, so that the truth of· "God is being" could be not only believed but experienced. Biblical theology and Greek ontology thus depended upon each other for the truth they could show. But this alliance has long since been broken. Theologically Schleiermacher widened the breach beyond repair by declaring that dogmatic theology had nothing in common with speculative, metaphysical theology and did not even need to pay heed to it.

But there is another dimension of the matter, one to which Heidegger and Georg Picht call attention. This is the problem of the identity of being itself. God got into metaphysics in the first place, Heidegger suggested in "The Onto-theo-logical Constitution of Metaphysics," because from Plato and Aristotle to Hegel and Nietzsche what was left unthought was the difference between the one that is "over all" in the sense of a single one presiding over all others (the highest being), *das Seiende als das Seiendste*, and the one that is "overall" in the sense of the general that is in all (the being of all entities). Metaphysics thinks the being (*Sein*), the "to-be-something," of that which is something (*das Seiende*) "in the unity . . . of the most general . . . and also in the unity . . . of totality, that is, of the one that is the highest over all" (p. 125). No difference is made between the universal and the supreme; *das Seiende* can mean *the* one that is supremely, or *anyone* that is at all. But the God identified with supreme being is not the true God; Heidegger suggests if philosophy is to recover, at a deeper level, the truth which once appeared but no longer appears in the metaphysical tradition, the first task is to think the difference as such. To do so requires more than contrasting God with being, or be-ing (*Sein*) with the one that is (*das Seiende*), for that contrast thinks of the two as a difference within being but not of the difference as such. To put Heidegger's point in other terms: It is not enough to think "God is *not* being." The task is to think the *not*, just the difference and nothing more. To do so is to prepare the way for a postmetaphysical thinking of the truth that formerly appeared in the metaphysical tradition. In banishing the supreme being, atheistic philosophy of today may be, as

Heidegger thought, closer to the Godhood of God than philosophical theism. "The God of the philosophers," Picht writes, "is irrevocably dead—but the truth of this God perhaps will rise again in a new form" ("Gott," p. 251).

The experience of truth is, then, in the first place a matter of seeing that the meaning understood in an assertion is the same as the reality of what it refers to, even while the difference between meaning and reality is upheld. The "is" of true judgments, therefore, expresses both the identity and the difference in the unity of meaning and the unity of reality. In such cases as that of Schleiermacher's *Christian Faith* and Hegel's *Science of Logic* (from which Heidegger takes his direction in "The Onto-theo-logical Constitution of Metaphysics") the experience of truth upon the name of "God" can become possible only if the forgotten difference (in Hegel) and the forgotten identity (in Schleiermacher) are made manifest. This recovery cannot be made, I think, within the experience of being—which is to say that "God is being" will prove to be no more true than "God is not being." For in the experience of being there remains unthought the possibility, within thinking, that it is not necessary to think that the necessity of thought is the same as the givenness of being, and the possibility, within being, that the one in all (being in general) is not the same as the one over all (the supreme being).

Seeing the identity in the difference is to experience truth. To have this experience with theological assertions requires that in some way the ascertaining of what is so must be distinguishable from understanding what is said and that there is a vantage point from which to see the identity in that difference. Similarly, to experience truth with the name "God" requires that there is a difference and an identity in the name and that from some standpoint we can see the endurance of same in the different. This conception of truth frees the discussion from enslavement to just one among the several variations of truth; namely, the empirico-scientific one. It allows one to accept the validity of the empirico-analytical criticism of theology without confining it to the terms in which it was expressed. Technically the empiricist critique in its early form, as expressed most provocatively by Alfred Ayer in *Language, Truth and Logic*, is refuted easily enough by the simple observation that it is based on a self-contradictory position. If only empirically verifiable statements make sense and can be true or false, then the position that only such statements make sense does not make sense and can be neither true nor false since it is not empirically verifiable; the contention that the only sensible statements are those which are empirically verifiable is not itself empirically verifiable, and therefore it is nonsense. Since that is so, we are left only with a choice of which nonsense to subscribe to.

Such a refutation, however correct, only strikes the surface of the criticism. There was, and is, a sound concern underneath, that of the possibility of experiencing truth in theological assertions at all. That we can distinguish between true and false statements about the empirical world is due *inter alia* to our being able to make a difference between understanding what a statement asserts and ascertaining what is so about the thing to which it refers. Theological assertions become suspect when they elude efforts to determine their truth by failing at the critical juncture to make the necessary difference between understanding what they mean and ascertaining whether they are so. "Truth does not reduce," as Pivčević remarks, "either to true propositions or to true statements, it involves an *experience* of truth; it would be incoherent to make a truth-claim in respect of p and at the same time deny that p could ever be seen to be the case, that anyone could ever say on the basis of own experience, 'That is how things are' " ("Truth," p. 319). The manner in which physical science ascertains what is so and thus verifies or falsifies its statements is but one way of determining identity in difference. There are other ways of doing so and hence other ways of experiencing the truth of assertions and things. What constitutes truth as such, however, is the structure of identity in difference, which can be reflectively seen.

The Structure of Reflection: Soul, Truth, and Time

The experiencing subject, which sees the identity in difference, is itself an identity in difference. Or, to put the matter differently, it is a point at which the two things that, in the experience of truth, correspond to each other actually converge with each other. To understand a meaning carried by linguistic signs, to perceive how objects are given to us, and to see that the meaning and the datum are the same are moments in the experience, which is made possible by the convergence, in the reflecting self, of the various elements. The "I" of reflection is what Heidegger called "being-in-the-world," or *Dasein*, and what in Aristotelian terminology is called the *anima*, the soul, which, as Thomas put it, is "ens quod natum est convenire cum omni ente," an entity whose nature it is to come together with every entity (*De ver.*, 1,1; Heidegger, *SuZ*, p. 14). Indeed, "the soul is, in a certain way, all things sensible and intelligible because in the soul are both sense and understanding or knowledge; and sense, moreover, is in a certain way the sensibles themselves, the understanding (*intellectus*) is the intelligibles or knowledge the knowables" (3 *Anim.*, 13a; Schütz, s.v.).

That is to say, it is "I" who can both understand meanings and ascertain facts, form thoughts and receive data, and it is "I" who make the comparison in reflection between the contents of both. It is in this "I" that all comes together. That Heidegger, in *Being and Time*, can call this "soul" *Dasein* is due to his having altered the metaphysical terminology so that the act which is directed toward being (what is other than thought) is itself called "being" instead of "thinking" and, correspondingly, the activity of "thinking of" (as in "thinking of death") is called "being toward" (*Sein zu*, as in *Sein zum Tode*). The "soul" or *Dasein* in the experience of truth is nothing other than the point of reflection where thinking and being come together. *Dasein* is the remoteness of being manifested in the closeness of "here," the *ecce homo* as a "here I am," just as *anima* is the unity of thinking and being. Every self capable of reflecting is a point at which there is such an identity of *intellectus* and *res*. Everyone so engaged is phenomenally an "absolute I" (in Fichte's language), a *Dasein*, an "eternal soul."

At the opposite end of the self-to-other relation is the identity of truth as such, the connectedness of meaning and reality in all entities that is seen in the experience of truth. Reflection and truth, or *anima* and *veritas*, are thus designations of the two ter-mini of the experience. At the root of the ontological demonstra-tion of God is the notion that the idea of God is truth, or that, just as soul is another name for the reflecting "I," "God" is another name for the truth as such. Unlike other conceptions, the idea of God is one in which meaning and reality not only agree with each other but actually converge. In the idea of God the meaning of the concept and the reality of the being come together; the idea of God *is* God—just as the *anima* is all entities. This is to say that the word "God" not only carries a sense but also is a datum, a real thing-there with which the mind must deal.

What is between these two identities (soul; truth) is not in turn either *Dasein* or truth but the reflective act of bringing meaning and being together through *projection* and *disclosure*. Understand-ing the meaning carried by signs (the visual or acoustic figures that we see on a page or hear spoken and that we call words) projects the reality indicated; and how the object shows itself makes it possible to ascertain the reality corresponding to the projection. This connection between projection (from the sign-sense) and ascertainment (from the disclosure) is neither the identity of the reflecting self nor that of truth; it is, rather, *time*.

This is made clear in Heidegger's analysis of an example of the experience of truth, the verification of the assertion "The paint-ing on the wall is hanging obliquely" (*SuZ*, pp. 218f.). The Aris-totelian view which Heidegger is correcting, though not by name, can be found in Anselm's *Monolog* (chap. 31), in which it is maintained that the degree of truth in an assertion depends upon how closely the likeness of the object in our mind "imitates the object of which it is the likeness" (p. 91). Truth, Heidegger writes, does not have "the structure of an agreement between cognition and object in the sense of an assimilation (*Angleichung*) of one entity (subject) to another (object)." To see that this is so, assume that someone, whose back is toward the wall, makes the assertion ("The painting is crooked") and that it is true. It is then verified through turning around and perceiving the crooked picture on the wall. That to which the assertion relates one is not a representation of the thing but the real painting on the wall. Making the assertion is itself a "Sein zum seienden Ding selbst," a relating of oneself in thought to the real thing itself; the projection it contains is not that of a representation of the object but of the object itself. What is shown in the verification, as one turns around to perceive the painting on the wall, is nothing else than that the picture is the entity that was meant in the assertion. What is verified is that the assertion about the entity does point out and disclose the entity to which the self related itself in thought. The entity shows itself to be in itself the same as how it is projected, or disclosed, in the assertion. What is between the *intellectus* and the *res* is the temporality indicated by saying—not in Heidegger's words—that the thing *is* in itself what it *was* in the assertion.

William James's pragmatic account of truth shows this temporality between the two, not like Heidegger from the side of the entity, but from the side of the working idea. Otherwise his account of what constitutes the verification of an assertion is similar to Heidegger's. In one of his examples James asks us to suppose that, while sitting in his library in Cambridge, Massachusetts, he thinks of Memorial Hall, a building that is a few minutes' walking time away. If, by means of his idea of the hall, he can lead us to the hall and tell us "of its history and present uses"; if in its presence he feels his idea, "however imperfect it may have been," to have "led hither and to be now terminated"; and if, finally, the terms of the image correspond to those of the felt hall "serially" in the progress from his library to the hall, then, he concludes, his idea "must be, and by common consent would be, called cognizant of reality." "The percept here not only *verifies* the concept, proves its function of knowing that percept to be true, but the percept's existence as the terminus of the chain of intermediaries *creates* the function. Whatever terminates that chain was, because it now proves itself to be, what the concept 'had in mind.' " James then asks, "Why not treat the working of the idea from next to next as the essence of its self-transcendency? Why insist that knowing is a static relation *out of time* when it practically seems so much a function of our active life?" (*Meaning*, pp. 105, 109, 120 [italics in the last added]).

A theory which construes truth to mean that a mental image and a perceived object look alike is not adequate because it is at best a form of truth derivative from the more basic one described in Heidegger's and James's examples. Not only does it overlook the timing of verification, it is also only one variation on the theme of identity in difference. A likeness-theory, which may sound plausible when applied to the mental image of a green leaf compared with the actual sight of it, cannot explain how we recognize the truth of assertions that do not have to do with picturable objects at all. We can, for example, recognize that the assertion " '*S* is *P*' is a judgment" is true without being able to form a mental picture of "*S* is *P*" as a judgment so as to make a comparison with "*S* is *P*" as a perceived object. Such a recognition indicates the defectiveness of a likeness-theory of truth. Similarity of appearance may indeed be a device employed to decide whether some assertions are true. Quite possibly the meaning of "The picture on the wall is hanging obliquely" is present to our mind as a mental image of a crooked picture on a wall. But the device so used as an aid in determining the truth of the assertion is not an account of the experience of truth. As James pointed out, if his concept can do all of the things mentioned, then it matters not at all whether he had a clear image or only a name for Memorial Hall. The temporality of reflection and being—that the concept leads to the percept and that the thing perceived shows itself to be the same as what was meant in the assertion—is an essential ingredient in the account of truth.

What the reflective subject sees in this experience is "truth," but what is between the soul and the truth is nothing other than time, the temporality that manifests itself in the process of verification. The formula "seeing the same in the different" may suggest the image of looking into two compartments and comparing their contents. This image, which may rightly serve as a picture of the experience, should not mislead one into thinking that the self-same content that appears in both partitions is a whole divided into two. It is, rather, like one and the same pigeon which appears in the first pigeonhole when we look there and in the second when we look there, and between the two is only time. The movement of the pigeon from the one to the other (time itself) cannot be seen, it is behind the wall, but it can be named, and it is manifested in the experience of seeing the same in the different. In this sense truth is a manifestation of temporality; truth is how time makes its appearance, the form in which it manifests itself, more originally than in the passage of minutes from past into the future. For that reason our experience of chronometric time is based upon our experience of truth, in which time as such is manifested.

The medium of this experience is language. Discourse, or *logos*, makes the projection of reality possible by its sign-character. Words in the flow of use are signs that carry a sense, the sense carries a significance, and the significance points to a referent. Thus "The leaf is green" bears a *sense* in that we can, for example, picture what it is saying. This meaning, in turn, has a *significance* inasmuch as we know that a green leaf belongs to the realm of physically perceptible objects rather than, say, among tonal relations. The sense and significance, in turn, point to a *referent*, a datum that can be given either in accord, or in discord, with how the reality is projected. It is also discourse that, from the other side, makes the disclosure possible by its capacity to show. Words are things that are thoughts, and as such thought-things they can show other things. We know, for example, that the word "tree" is not a tree and yet it is of the tree inasmuch as it shows the object, to which it refers, as a tree. Language is, in short, the medium in which the experience of truth takes place, a role it can play because it is itself an identity in difference.

As a piece of language, an assertion contains an identity of sign and sense; the visual or acoustic figure (a tactile one in the case of Braille) carries its own sense. But we can distinguish the sense from the sign. Thus, we can recognize that "tree" and "Baum" are visually as well as acoustically two different signs although they carry the same sense. "Big dipper" is one sign with two different senses, depending on whether it indicates something in the kitchen or something in the sky and whether it is literally or metaphorically understood. There is a similar identity in difference between the sign-sense and the significance and reference it contains. "Equilateral triangle" and "equiangular triangle" are two partly different signs containing two different senses, yet they project the same figure. Again, the sense of "The desk has a yellow pencil on it" (where we are saying something about the desk) is different from that of "A yellow pencil is on the desk" (where we are saying something about a pencil); nonetheless, the real state of affairs projected by the two is one and the same.

The synthesis of understanding and reality, of meaning and being, which is implicit in the experience of truth is, on closer analysis, a synthesis of two syntheses. Meaning (sense) is the synthesis of singular and universal, subject and predicate, that makes up the concept of the whole assertion. It is the unitary sense that we understand through the sense-bearing linguistic signs. Thus, the meaning of the judgment "This is a tree," which distinguishes and combines the three elements of subject, predicate, and copula, is the sense of the whole sentence. The Latin word for this, *intellectus*, is to be taken not as "idea" or "thought" but as the whole sense of the verbal signs and also as the capacity to understand such senses. "Understanding" in English has the same double signification; one's understanding is what one understands (meaning) as well as the capacity to understand. In other words, the meaning of an assertion is neither its subject nor its predicate alone or added together but precisely the unity of the two that is their synthesis.

Reality (*res*) is a similar synthesis of singular and universal in the object to which the meaning refers. The reality of an object is neither the singular percept nor the abstract thought but precisely the connection between the two. It is the unity we ascertain in how a thing presents itself to us. Thus, the reality of a tree is not its being there nor its treehood but the unity of the two in the whole object as perceptible and cognizable. Meaning and reality are coordinate; the one is a synthesis of understanding which either coincides with or conflicts with the other as a synthesis of the object.

Both the unity of meaning and that of reality are indicated by the "is" of judgments ("This is a tree"). Hence Aquinas could say (*S.th.*, 1,3,4,2) that the verb "to be" is used in two ways—to signify the act of being and to signify the mental uniting of predicate and subject in a proposition. Accordingly, neither a photograph nor a phantasm of a tree is, as such, the same as an image or representation of the "being" of the tree, either as meaning or as reality. Only an image or representation that manifests the hidden connection between the two elements of perceptibility and cognizability, singular and universal, is a portrayal of the object's "being" rather than of its perception or notion. Indirectly reality and meaning appear in the experience of truth as the two syntheses of singular and universal that are seen to be the same in the different.

These several relations can be fixed in the following terminology: A *concept* is the connection of singular and universal in a thought. Thus the concept of a tree is the thought of "this (= the thing in view) *as* a tree," a unity of concrete percept and abstract thought. The meaning of a proposition, or judgment, is always a concept. That, in the thing, which corresponds to a concept is *reality*, the real connection between the two elements that are brought together in the concept. The identity of concept and reality is expressed by *being*—the "is" of the copula and the "is" of the thing as it shows itself. *Truth* is the identity of being (or of not being) in the midst of the difference between the concept and the reality.

Truth, as has been stated, is a matter of reflective experience, which is intertwined with, but distinguishable from, the direct experience of mundane objects (literal experience). But if reflection is distinct from literal experience, it is also distinct from reflexivity. It is located between the literal and the reflexive. The nature of the distinction can most readily be made clear by a set of paradigms, word-models of the acts and corresponding experiences.[4]

Literal experience—the kind involved in physical objects and literal words—can be represented by the paradigms

    (1) "This is a tree"

    (2) " 'This is a tree' is a judgment"

Paradigm (1) embodies an act of object-relatedness; it results from and expresses a consciousness of the being of a mundane object. Paradigm (2) embodies an act of self-relatedness; it expresses a consciousness of the being of a mental act.[5]

Reflective experience is shown in the paradigm

    (3) " 'This is a tree' is true"

This kind of redoubled judgment shows how reflective objects appear in, but are distinct from, direct objects. It expresses a consciousness of reflective objects (phenomena).

A fourth paradigm can be formed for reflexivity, so as to show both its connection to object-consciousness and reflection and also its reflexive character:

    (4) " ' "This is a tree" is true' is true"

The sense of this paradigm is that a true statement about the object is also a true statement about reflection.[6] It expresses reflexive self-consciousness. Reflexive assertions are used in normal discourse even more rarely than reflective ones. Indeed, at first blush they seem not only artificial but superfluous. F.P. Ramsey ("Facts," p. 17) even thought that "It is true" is a "superfluous addition" to any statement on the grounds that it does not say any more than the original true statement. All the more might one argue that "It is true that it is true that this is a tree" says nothing more about the relation between thought and reality than does "It is true that this is a tree." Yet the sentence does distinguish reflexivity from reflection and from object-consciousness. And just as Strawson, after arguing against Ramsey that "It is true" adds a performance to true statements—it enacts agreement with them—later granted, in reply to criticisms, that "at least part" of what saying a statement is true does is "to make a statement about a statement" ("Problem," p. 69), so too this reflective dimension opens to reflexivity. " ' "This . . ." is true' is true" is a paradigm, not for the experience of reflective objects, but for the experience of reflection itself. For purposes of direct and reflective experience such a wording is redundant because reflection is not normally *what* we experience but the means by which we experience such phenomena as truth.

The reflexive relation is, in the language of speculative idealism, an "absolute" one inasmuch as the experienced phenomenon (reflection) is of the same kind as are the experiencing act (reflecting) and the origin of the experience (self-reflection). This circularity is what gives reflexivity and the linguistic paradigm that formulates it their apparent emptiness and superfluity. One might dismiss reflexivity from further consideration as an unnecessary duplication except that it is inevitably the court to which conflicts between religion and reflection are first taken. Moreover, it is also used for testing the universalizability of a position, as Plato showed in *Cratylus* (385-387). An example of its employment appeared above in connection with the empirico-analytical critique of theological statements. If that empiricism is made into a position, instead of being taken as a heuristic method or a device, it defeats itself, for its principle, which states that only statements which are verifiable through sense perception are sensible statements, cannot be applied to itself without being shown to be nonsensical by its own standard. Reflexivity is used in order to show that the empiricist principle, which can be applied to other assertions but not to itself, always has at least one exception. With the definition of truth as identity in difference, by contrast, an appeal to reflexivity confirms the universalizability. The definition is true by the same standard it enunciates—if what it says about truth is the same as and different from what truth is.

In paradigms (1) and (2) the word "this" denotes an object or act before our eyes or mind. To see a thing *as* a tree or to see words *as* the product of an act is to take cognizance of them as the object and product they are; and to judge that a thing *is* a tree and that a set of words *is* a judgment is to know them as such and thereby to complete the cognition.

In paradigm (3) the relation to the literal object is indirect; for reflective thought is not about a thing but about a relation between the thing and the thought of the thing. The thing is still indirectly present, of course; for if we did not understand "This is a tree" at all, we would not understand the meaning of " 'This is a tree' is true" either. Nevertheless, the other term of the relation in reflection is not the thing there but the relation between it and our consciousness of it. The referent of "This is a tree" is a physical object; the referent of " 'This . . .' is a judgment" is a mental act (which itself is a relation to an object); but the referent of " 'This . . .' is true" is the reflective object "truth," which appears in the relation between the first act and its object.

Finally, in paradigm (4) the original object (the tree) has virtually disappeared from view. Direct consciousness, which has as its other term a thing present, gives way to reflection,[7] in which the other term is a foregoing relation to an object or a product; as reflexivity takes over, the other term of the relation is the preceding reflection, so that reflexivity must be described, exactly but inelegantly, as a relation to the relation-to-the-relation (reflection) to the object or act (direct consciousness).

In this account of the structure of experience, *religion* (as the consciousness of an appearing deity) belongs on the plane of literal consciousness. Indeed that is how religion as such enters experience. It does not yet explicitly involve the *anima* (being-in-the-world, the I) and truth (the phenomenon of identity in difference). Thus, as a religious assertion, "God exists" is on a par with the empirical assertion "This is a tree" and the personal one "That is John"; it has the sense of "The one there is God." *Philosophy of religion*, by contrast, belongs on the plane of reflection. Its assertions are not those of a first-order relation to God (or to whatever the direct object of religious consciousness is called) but those of a second-order relation to that relation. *Theology*, when related to religion, can oscillate between the two. Sometimes it has the character of philosophy of religion; at other times it is religious thought.

To religious consciousness philosophy of religion appears as a denial of religion when it raises the question of truth because that question rejects the unconditional quality of the relation to the one named "God." This is a point that philosophy of religion, with such exceptions as Tillich's "Religionsphilosophie," generally ignores. It is, however, recognized in Thomas Altizer's *Self-Embodiment of God*—"the utterance of the name of God makes . . . visible, or audible, the final exile of actuality from eternal presence" (p. 30). Reflection on the truth of religion is possible only at the cost of the literal religious consciousness. To reflect on it, and thus to bring the soul out of its unreflected identity with the subjective consciousness, is to have "fallen" from the primary relation to the deity. For that reason Barth could write in the first edition of his commentary on Paul's Epistle to the Romans, "Reflection (*Selbstschau*), 'human knowledge', 'experience'. . . — all of that is possible only *outside* God . . . , [it is] sin, it does *not* essentially belong to man" (*Rb* [1], pp. 128-129). The standpoint of reflection, from which one sees the truth that appears unreflected in direct experience, seems incapable of showing the truth of religion. To contend that a relation to God can be reflected as can a relation to an object is to deny that God is as unconditional as he appears to be in the religious relation.

The competing claims of religion and reflection, where the one (religion) says the other is sin—not really reflection but a mask for the denial of religion—and where the other (reflection) says that the first is an illusion, cannot be adjudicated by reflection and religion themselves; each sees the other differently from how the other sees itself, and each can explain the existence of the other in a way satisfactory to itself but unacceptable to the other. Religion views the possibility of reflection as a fall into sin and warns against it; reflection sees religion as a prereflective state which needs deliverance from its illusion. Each, in the judgment of the other, is blind to its own nature. This unresolved conflict is one of the basic determinants of intellectual and spiritual life today, as it has been since the beginning of the nineteenth century.

A solution must appeal initially to reflexivity as a standpoint from which the conflict can be seen independently of how the two contenders see it. But the appeal puts reflection into a greater dilemma than is often recognized. If one rejects the appeal to reflexivity, reflection takes on a religious character by exempting itself from its own critique and thus setting itself up as a pseudoreligion. But if one does not reject the appeal, reflection may learn that the phenomenon of truth, which it experiences and which it finds lacking in religion, is a penultimate phenomenon pointing in turn to something that lies beyond truth and falsehood as well as beyond truth and illusion. Reflection thus risks its own character upon becoming reflexivity as much as does religion upon becoming reflection.

Nineteenth-century speculative idealism undertook to make this turn to reflexivity by reference to the idea of God. When turned upon the idea of God, in which meaning and reality converge, reflection becomes reflexive in such a way that it is speculation, a mirroring of the nature and movement present in the idea—identical with the reality—of God himself. In speculative reflexivity the process by which reflection normally determines truth—seeing whether a meaning and a datum are in agreement with each other—becomes a reenactment of the life that is present in the reality. That is to say, in a thought on the order of "This is a tree" what is intended is being; in " 'This . . .' is true" the intention is meaning in being; and in " ' "This . . ." is true' is true" it is the meaning in the meaning of being. But the thought of the meaning in the meaning in being is the mirror (*speculum*) and reenactment of the activity of the being of the Trinitarian God. In this way the sense of a reflexive proposition corresponds to the being of God; and "God is truth" says the same as " ' "This . . ." is true' is true," as a mirror reflection shows (with a certain inversion) the same as the entity it reflects. When reflexivity sees itself as such a mirroring of the divine life, it sees truth not only in a correspondence between meaning and reality but also in the coming together of its convergence (the *anima*, the reflecting I) with that of the idea-reality "God."

This idealism suffered the fate of being both misunderstood at its time and forgotten subsequently. It was misunderstood because it did not fit into the alternative of dogmatic and critical, supranatural and rational, religious and reflective, which was prevalent not only in schematizing but also in understanding theological positions. To the critical, speculative idealism appeared orthodox; to the orthodox, it appeared critical; and to both, it appeared suspect because it undermined the basic alternative which sustained both parties in their mutual opposition. Later when it became clear that this idealism had not finally overcome the hiatus between meaning and reality, it was easier for others to remember that speculative idealism had failed than to understand what it was or why it had done so. Speculative idealism recognized that in theology, as that discipline's name and origin suggest, truth must be more than a correspondence perceptible to reflection; it must be a convergence between reflection and God's being or, if one will, between the soul's thinking and speaking of God and God's own thinking and speaking. But this idealism could not carry out its own demand.

In "Über den Logos" (1833), an essay that marks the culmination of speculation as well as a turn from idealism to linguistic phenomenology, Karl Daub formulated the problem, which he still thought speculative thinking could handle, thus: The self expressed in the pronoun "I" is an identity of thought and its corresponding object such that any self is not only conditioned by the determinations of singular, particular, and universal (I am this, particular, and human entity) but is also the source or principle of those determinations (it is "I" who think in terms of such distinctions and understand them by reference to subjectivity).[8] In that sense the self is the "category of all categories." Thinking and knowing are always done by a subject about an object. The demand to give up my self for the sake of some other kind of knowing (in which the subject and object are transcended) is on the face of it impossible to fulfill. For *me* to demand that I give up my self is self-contradictory; *I* demand it, even though I demand it of myself, and insofar as I demand, I do not give up my place of priority at all. It is equally contradictory for another to make the demand of me since the other would have to show me the necessity of doing so; and insofar as *I* then decide whether the demonstration has succeeded, I do not give up my capital position at all ("Logos," pp. 355-356).

The Jeopardy in Standpoint

Reflexivity is the place to which the conflict between religion and critique leads experience. But the conflict between the reflective and the literal, of which this is a part, is complicated by conflicts in literal experience itself, which spring from the factor of standpoint. This important, but easily confused, matter requires a somewhat extended account here.

The very awareness of the reflective experience of phenomena as comprised in and yet distinct from the experience of objects and meanings brings with it the possibility of reckoning with diverse points of view. For reflection involves a doubling of the subject. Not only can one reflectively compare meanings with realities, one can also distinguish the world-related, first-order subject from the reflective one, the former being part of the relation to a thing or meaning and the latter a part of the relation to that relation. The first-order, unreflective subject can thus be seen as one which may experience an object in its meaning (the two elements so intimately joined in language that every thing has only one name) but which does not experience truth as such. An unreflective subject cannot, for example, compare a present with a past experience of an object so as to distinguish between appearance and reality. Since such a subject is always directly influenced by the object before it, it is completely absorbed in its momentary experiences. To it a stick lying half in the water not only appears to be, but is, bent, for the difference between how a thing appears and how it is does not even arise. After the stick has been taken out of the water, it is no longer bent; it is other than what it was before. If a subject, however, is aware of the past in relation to the present, it is already beginning to reflect; distinguishing between what a thing is and what it was is already a work of reflection. To the extent, therefore, that time enters language reflection is already on the threshold.

Our conception of an unreflective subject is, admittedly, an abstraction from actual human being. No one may ever have been totally unreflective toward objects. But we can form a conception of the unreflective state of mind which precedes reflection because for all of us there are still areas of experience which remain relatively unreflected. Thus, whereas everyone is aware that a stick when it lies submerged has another appearance than when no part of it is under water, most of us do not attend to the variation in how a coin appears in a purse and how it appears on a counter. Similarly, whereas we may attend to the difference between the percept and the thought in "this tree" when we deliberate about it, we do not make such a distinction in everyday conversation and dealings; whereas we can distinguish meanings of words from the things to which they refer, we take the signing of a contract to mean indifferently that the parties agree upon the meaning of the words and that they agree upon carrying out the actions the meaning intends. Reflectively one sees such differences, unreflectively not.

Reflectively one can also distinguish points of view from each other so as to be able to speak of perspective in the apprehension of an object. Looking at a tree from the north we see one aspect, from the south another; the change in point of view provides us with different appearances of the object but it does not imply that the object itself has changed. To confirm the fact that it was our point of view and not the tree which changed we take at least two first-order subjects into account in the relation to the object. The different aspects of the tree, which from the point of view of one moving subject could be regarded either as a change in the object or as an alteration of a subject's location, now is read as the latter. One viewer on the north side and one on the south of the same thing can compare their two different perceptions of it. Thus, the emergence of reflection makes possible a distinction not only between reflective and first-order subjects but also between one and another first-order subject.

Furthermore, this recognition is the basis of our being able to distinguish between conceiving what the object is and *ascertaining* it to be what we have conceived it to be. For the difference between conceiving the being of an object (when, for example, we form the judgment "This is a tree") and ascertaining its reality (confirming that it is indeed a tree) rests not only, as shown previously, upon the ability to compare the meaning of words and the being of the object by way of the projection contained in the meaning and the manifestation of being in the thing, but also, as we now see, upon the execution of two different first-order, or literal, relations to the thing. In conceiving, we are referred directly to the object itself; in ascertaining, the same is the case. But between the two comes the distinguishing of the meaning understood from the reality intended. From this time on the "truth" of a matter has to do with what presents itself to us not merely from one point of view but from the greatest number or, at least, from that point of view which most fully reveals what the object in itself, or in its own perspective, really is. Each ascertainment of a reality can in its turn become the starting concept for a further ascertainment; that is the process of verification. We judge that "this is a tree" and ascertain the judgment to be true by taking another point of view upon it; that ascertainment can subsequently be our starting concept for a further test. As long as one can find points of view not yet taken, this process can continue without becoming idly repetitive.

Related to the notion of point of view is that of standpoint. Standpoints are most prominent in what are called "value-judgments." Although the whole of value theory has fallen into disrepute, the notion of value, if cautiously used, is still legitimate and necessary. As an illustration of a value-judgment one may consider the difference between "Caesar was an honorable man" and "Caesar was assassinated on the Ides of March." If someone we may call M makes the latter assertion and another one called N denies it, then not both of them can be stating the truth; and the fact that Caesar was assassinated on that day in March can be determined regardless of M's and N's attitudes toward the Roman emperor.

But the statement "Caesar was an honorable man" is another matter. Here the subjectivity of M and N comes into play as a codeterminant of the character of the man; for honorability cannot be measured except through an impression made upon M and N by the person in question. Even this disagreement may be adjudicable if we stipulate that an honorable man is one who does x, y, and z. Then if Caesar did x, y, and z, he was an honorable man. But neither M nor N is likely to be satisfied with such a settlement, for they do not regard themselves as arguing about the definition of a term but about the character of a person. Whether he is seen to be honorable is partly determined by the subjectivity of the disputants, but this does not mean the argument concerns only how the terms are understood. M and N are, rather, themselves measuring instruments of the quality, or value, in dispute.

That is to say, value-judgments, far from being mere expressions of subjective opinion, are capable of being true or false, despite the fact that their truth cannot be determined in disregard of the subjective factor. When this is recognized, such disagreements cannot be dealt with merely by clarification of terms or by declaring that what is true for one may be false for another. Of course, some apparent disagreements about values may vanish when terms are clarified. But real disagreements are not terminological. Thus, when a pollster inquires of historians how they rank American presidents as to greatness, the assumption is that the results will indicate something about the presidents and not only about the historians. So too the truth of whether Caesar was indeed an honorable man, though it cannot be seen apart from the impressions made upon M and N, is a matter of whether he did have a certain quality. In truth he was either honorable or not.

How is the truth of value-judgments determined? One means that might suggest itself is to employ the notion of points of view. Just as one gains a three-dimensional view of a tree or some other object by successively observing it from points all around and fusing the views into one; just as Monet's succession of twenty impressionist paintings of the west door of the Cathédrale de Rouen under the changing light of morning, noon, and evening and of various seasons can be fused into one variegated impression of the façade, so too the impressions made upon M and N by Caesar can be fused into a whole view of the character of the man. Thus one might think M's impression of Caesar as an honorable man and N's opposite impression form two points of view, the whole truth lying in a perspective which incorporates Caesar's honorability (as seen from the side of M's value-system) and dishonorability (as seen from the side of N's).

Yet the difficulty of applying the notion of point of view here is that the disputants do not see different aspects of a single character. We can say that a tree is both light (on one side) and dark (on another) without losing a unitary picture of the tree; through all of Monet's twenty paintings of the cathedral of Rouen, a viewer does not lose sight of the fact that it is the same building appearing in different lightings and that the qualities it displays are not incompatible with each other. But is it possible to compose one impression out of honorable and dishonorable as we can form a single phantasm out of successive views of an object? Is it possible for M to think of N simply as looking at Caesar from another side and to be able to concede that viewed in one way Caesar was honorable but viewed in another he was contemptible? Not if M does mean what he said when he asserted that Caesar *was* an honorable man. The disagreement between M and N derives not from points of view but from standpoints—one can alter one's point of view, but not one's standpoint, without becoming a different person. The subjective factor in value judgments, which makes determining their truth so difficult, is a matter of standpoint—of "existential" or "personal" standpoint—and not merely of points of view.

A debate concerning the truth of a value-judgment may have either of two outcomes. In the example cited, the historical figure Julius Caesar cannot really have been both as M sees him and as N sees him to have been. But a poet, a maker of images, may produce a historical novel or play containing a figure called Julius Caesar who is convincingly human and displays a quality of which we had not been aware before, one that precisely combines our impressions of honorable and dishonorable. The name of that figure may then become a new adjective in our language—"Julianic" (in analogy to "quixotic"). With the creation of such a figure the disagreement between M and N can conceivably be settled and the truth of their disparate judgments seen; each can now see that that is the predicate most suitable. Initially both cannot be right in their conflicting value-assertions, but with the new predicate, they may be able to regard their impressions as comparable to two points of view which have been brought together in the notion of "Julianic." This outcome is made possible if the figure created is capable of impressing M and N as the true Caesar whose personal quality breaks out of the alternative of honorable and dishonorable that had been set by previous experience as embodied in language. M and N can then revise their earlier judgments as incomplete.

A second possible outcome is that the "Julianic" figure so depicted remains only fictional, a figure one might meet in a play but not in the actual life or history of the person under dispute. When that happens, M and N can regard the fictional portrait as a poetic image, showing the possibility of truth behind their conflicting impressions of Caesar without, however, enabling them to alter their direct impressions of the man who historically was Julius Caesar. Their impressions in such a case result not from points of view but from personal standpoints. That is to say, in view of the historical figure (as mediated by whatever records still exist) M can only say, "Caesar was an honorable man," and "It is true that Caesar was an honorable man." He can see truth in the fictional portrait only as a nonliteral, artistic truth and only to the extent that the fictional person shows how the one Julius

Caesar can be the two things he is to M and N. Such a portrait reveals a hidden historical person, a possibility one can envision but not identify with the actual impression the person makes. It presents a correspondence between what is seen from the two incompatible standpoints, but it does not alter the result of the literal experience of that person as mediated by the historical records. The hidden dimension lies between the real Caesar who appears to M and the real Caesar of N. Its appearance in a work of productive imagination does not cancel the incompatibility of M's and N's literal impressions of the historical figure, nor does it change the fact that each impression may be verified on its own by its holder if the other is disregarded.

Any disagreement, then, in value-judgments of the kind illustrated may have either of these two outcomes—a third value may be created which embraces the two different ones on their own level, as "Julianic" might comprise Brutus's and Anthony's impressions of Julius Caesar, or one may be created which presents the figure hidden in the historical person. In the latter case "hiddenness" means what it does in the phrase "the hidden God"—an imaginable or credible possibility that is associated with an actuality where it cannot be literally seen, as when divine omnipotence is revealed as hidden in the death of Jesus. At the outset we do not know which kind of solution is possible in given controversies over values. The opposition may be owing to a limitation of language and the experience built into it, or it may arise from incompatibility between existential standpoints, the nature of which is that any given human subject can make only one of two conflicting assessments in first-order relations to the value. The portrait of Jesus as the Christ, about which Tillich remarks that "Christianity acknowledges the paradox [that a defeated Messiah is not a Messiah at all]—and accepts it" (*ST*, 2, p. 111), is a portrait of such a hidden truth behind the value "Messiah." That is to say, in a literal relation we can see as true either that Jesus was the Messiah or that he was not, but it is not possible to see both as true. Yet the picture drawn of Jesus as Christ in Tillich's christology and indicated by this quotation is a hidden portrait of the truth behind the two standpoints toward the Messiahship of Jesus.

To test the truth of an assertion about hidden portraits, reflection must see whether the personal standpoint is both validated and also limited as a standpoint by the portrait itself. Hidden truth appears as the correspondence not between understanding (of meaning) and ascertainment (of reality) alone but between the truth that can be seen from one standpoint and the truth from another by two different subjects. Difference of point of view (when we are dealing with a physical object) always implies only that the viewing position may change while the perceiving apparatus, our sensory equipment, remains the same and, furthermore, that the perceiving apparatus is the same for any human subject. But differences in evaluation (as, e.g., regarding the honorability of a man) come not from varying locations of a neutral subject but from subjective differentiation. With respect to values a reflective subject must be able to do more than compare meanings as he or anyone understands them and realities as he or anyone ascertains them, from a variety of points of view; he must also be able to compare his own results, regarded as the truth from one standpoint, with those of other standpoints. But to do this he is dependent upon a second subject *who he can never be*, but who serves as a second measuring device through which truth appears. That we can do this second reflection implies the development of a consciousness different from that of an object-related subject as well as from that of a reflective but neutral observer.

Standpoint As a Problem in Science

The factor of standpoint is not peculiar to theology or, generally, to value-judgments. Indeed, it has entered the most objective of world-sciences—physics. Until recently it was not considered necessary to take account of the possibility of standpoint in the sciences because the scientific method required the neutralization of all standpoints and owed its successes to just that neutralization. The method of abstracting from all factors of differentiation in the human subject in favor of those in principle common to all was thought to be the method by which to arrive at the truth of things. Anyone capable of performing a given experiment will arrive at the same results as any other experimenter since the experimental discipline abstracts from the personal history, character, wishes, and the like, which might make one person see things differently from another. In this classical conception of science the truth of assertions is ideally independent of all particular standpoints. Standpoint has not, strictly speaking, been eliminated, but it has been universalized. What is true is so for *any* knowing subject rather than for *no* subject. Objectivity, said Kant, is universal subjectivity. The background of the ideal of a universal subject is doubtless theological—to know things as they really are is to know them as God knows them from a divine standpoint. Nevertheless, the scientific method does not depend upon that background for its working.

The limitation in this conception, which was exposed by the advent of quantum mechanics in the first decade of the present century and the development of quantum theory after 1915, is noteworthy here because it shows how recent physics is faced with the problem of standpoint. In an essay from the early 1930s the physicist Werner Heisenberg drew the conclusion that a sharp division of the world into subject and object was no longer possible and that, accordingly, the completely isolated object no longer had any describable properties ("Kausalgesetz," p. 182). This is to say that in dealing with microphysical particles no neutralized or standpoint-free approach can be adopted. Specifically, the question had to do with the measurement of position and velocity of elementary particles. These particles are affected by the measuring apparatus in such a way that it is impossible to determine both the position and the velocity of a particle, and this impossibility results not from temporary deficiencies but from ineradicable limitations. No refinement of apparatus will make it possible to measure experimentally both the position and the velocity of a given particle or set of particles.[9]

In effect, therefore, quantum physics must reckon with a factor analogous to that of standpoint. Granted, it is not the physicist but the measuring apparatus that determines the standpoint, conditioning the results; that is of no methodological consequence, for it still entails that the theoretical physicist, as over against the experimentalist, is comparable to a reflective subject over against two first-order subjects, from each of which he receives part of his information; and neither of the two first-order subjects is able to measure both qualities of the physical object. Microphysical realities, like values, show themselves differently to first-order subjects because they are affected by the measuring activity of those subjects. This brings out a feature of standpoints that, as we have already noticed, distinguishes them from points of view—standpoints cannot be successively occupied and their results fused into one first-order object in the world. However, since it is a measuring apparatus and not the personal qualities of the experimenter that influences the behavior of the microphysical particles, we are not justified in concluding that in quantum physics scientific judgments have become the same as value judgments. We are justified only in concluding that a factor of standpoint is involved in quantum mechanics; just this is what constitutes a revolution over against the classical notion of objectivity, for it exposes a dimension of reality that is accessible only by a constructive reflection which puts together the incompatible results of the first-order relations to the world.

In theology the importance and intractability of standpoint are even greater. Whereas an electron's behavior is not affected by the attitudes of a physicist, how God appears may well be affected by what we believe God to be. This possibility has long been recognized. But only in the last century has the full weight of the variety of standpoints come to be recognized (often under the title of "pluralism," a somewhat inexact but useful concept). This recognition has not only altered the relation between religious or theological traditions; it has also, for example, attuned the ears of Luther scholars to passages neglected, such as the remark in the *Large Catechism* that God and faith *gehören zuhauf*, "belong to the same pile." An even more stunning phrase occurs in the lectures of 1531 on the Epistle to the Galatians, where Luther calls faith the *creatrix divinitatis* in us (see H.M. Barth, "Fides," pp. 89-106). Although the phrase occurs only there, the theme is recurrent. "What one considers God to be, how one believes and represents him, that is also how he is." Indeed, "fidere et credere macht Gott," "trusting and believing makes God." Furthermore, Luther regards faith as conditioning our view of mundane reality as well. In another place he remarks, "The unreligious have the sun, moon, earth, waters, air, and all terrestrial things, but because they are unreligious, not religious, therefore the sun is not the sun, the moon, earth, water, and air are not what they are" (*WA*, 40,1,36,8). Whether things "are what they are" depends upon whether the person who has them is *pius* or *impius*. For the unreligious they are impure and harmful things; for the religious they are good and beneficial. It is not only that the "natural" and the "evangelical" views of God and the world differ but that the standpoint in each case conditions what one sees as the reality: "Outside faith God loses his righteousness, glory, riches, etc., and there is nothing of majesty and divinity where there is no faith" (*WA*, 40,1,360,5-7).

The "natural man" does not recognize that the way he sees God is not true to God. Indeed, the fact is that the way he sees God *is* true to God in the relation in which God appears to him. Such a one sees God as wrathful, unjust, and punitive; as he "considers, believes, and imagines God to be," so is God as well. God shows himself to be what one thinks him to be. The disjunctive effect of faith, accordingly, is not to be thought of as simply distinguishing the true from the false; for what the "natural man" believes of God is in fact true of God—God *is* a wrathful avenger. Faith disjoins the religious (the biblical) from the unreligious (the natural) and the loving from the wrathful God, but this is not a separation of truth from falsehood. Just as the unreligious are human beings as much as are the religious, so the wrathful God is as much God as is the loving one. From the standpoint of the gospel, it can be seen that things "are not what they are" when viewed naturally; they have not yet manifested their being. But from the natural standpoint this cannot be seen.

With a glance forward to Feuerbach we can see the line of thought that is opened with these remarks. In the view indicated by Luther's statements (regardless of whether they are interpreted as formulating *the* view of Luther on theology) the "natural man" does not know that he is seeing things only on their surface; from his standpoint they do show themselves to be as he thinks they are. Nevertheless, the standpoint of the gospel shows the natural apprehension to be one which in principle has been overtaken by faith. The natural apprehension of the world and God is faith's past tense—not simply false but true in the past tense; it sees God always as he *was* but never as he *is* or will be, though it does not know of the preterit quality of its view. Thus the natural fear of God, reaching its apex in terror at the prospect of hell, is true, when seen from the standpoint of *fides*, only and always in the past tense. Hell is an image of that damnation from which deliverance has always already been accomplished.

However, if the standpoint so conditions the realities viewed that the one who occupies it does not know he is seeing only their surface or their superseded past, then Feuerbach can rightly take a step further, in order to argue that the standpoint of critique is to that of faith what faith was relative to the natural view. Indeed, Feuerbach makes a target of Luther's theology by name, contending that whereas it seems at first to be anything but an implicit anthropology, in the end it turns out to be just that—the highest exaltation of humankind, a covert belief in the divinity of the human species. One who understands himself radically as a sinner, and Christ radically as a redeemer, finds the certainty of redemption from sin and death; but this certainty, Feuerbach holds, is nothing else than the certainty of one's own divinity (*Wesen des Glaubens*, p. 366). Since faith in salvation is the same as faith in God, the certainty of one's own salvation is the same as the acknowledgement of the deity of one's own species. Feuerbach could thus say of religion very much the same as what

Luther had said of the natural mind—its view of things is not untrue, but true in the past tense.

In Luther's analysis the natural way of viewing does not recognize that it is a standpoint at all until it is overtaken by the fiducial view. Feuerbach goes further. The fiducial view likewise does not recognize itself as a standpoint until it is taken up into the critical view. But if, from the standpoint of *fides*, we see natural appearances as belonging in principle to the past ("by nature" we always see things as they were and never as they are and will be) without in turn recognizing that faith might be a standpoint equally oblivious of itself as such, and if, like Feuerbach's "anthropologian" (to coin a word combining anthropologist and theologian), we can see *fides* as always the preterit for critical consciousness, without being able to recognize that critique likewise is a standpoint, then what is to prevent us from anticipating still another standpoint from which critique, *fides*, and the natural thought can all be related to each other as a sequence of past tenses?

These questions indicate both the importance and the difficulty of standpoint for the experience of truth. We cannot straightaway speak of God as though we could occupy a neutral standpoint analogous to classical science. If the standpoint taken determines what we see and if we cannot disengage the standpoint from the objectival element in what we ascertain, how are we to experience the truth as truth and not as opinion? With the advent of faith in the sense indicated in the citations from Luther we have a disjunction of human subjects such that the objective term of the relation (God) is never given neutrally. Faith and nature both stand in direct relation to God, the one perceiving him to be of one kind, the other of another kind. Admittedly, faith can see both its own truth and that of natural apprehension, whereas the natural view can see faith only as false. In this sense *fides praesupponit naturam*—faith presupposes nature—not according to the formula "fides non tollit sed perficit naturam," "faith does not destroy but perfects nature," but according to the formula "fides tollit et tollens perficit naturam," "faith takes up and, by taking up, perfects nature." Furthermore, the Luther-like disjunction of faith and natural perception can be radicalized so as to include a Barthian or Tillichian disjunction between nihilism (nothing can ultimately resist human will) and faith in the wholly other God (for which nihilism is eternal truth in the past tense).

Nonetheless, this *fides* cannot rule out the possibility that it too is a standpoint. By taking up, as its own past, the natural perception of God, evangelical faith is able to see God in the whole truth of his eternal past and present; dialectical faith can do the same with nihilism. But can the God who appears to faith become the past tense for another standpoint, as Feuerbach suggested and Nietzsche's madman declared? Can dialectical faith, seen from another standpoint, be exposed as a mask for nihilism? From what standpoint can we adjudicate the different standpoints from which the objectival is perceived? Do we take an evolutionary view of human history so as to regard the latest standpoint (which will be recognized as such only when it is superseded) as the one from which all standpoints, recognized as such, are aligned? If so, is such an evolutionary conception itself merely a standpoint? Is there a position, not itself a standpoint, from which we can see all standpoints? From what position might one, for example, ascertain that religious belief in God gives way to belief in humanity, belief in humanity gives way to belief in being, and belief in being gives way to faith in being-itself, but faith in being-itself is nothing else than the completion of the process which started as belief in God and was propelled by the question of its own truth?

That we cannot appeal to an objective science to answer such questions is by now clear. For the theoretical physicist and the reflective theologian are in structurally similar positions. A theoretical physicist cannot view elementary particles in isolation from an experimental standpoint. He can "see" the nature of a particle only by relating to each other the separate deliverances of two experimental physicists, and he is subject to the question whether his theoretical view, even his mathematical formalism, is in its turn only a standpoint. Furthermore, in any given case the separate deliverances are not of equal valency. If an experimentalist chooses to measure position, he forfeits every opportunity to measure the velocity of the particle under investigation. To the theoretical physicist, therefore, the nature of the particle as comprising both its position and its velocity can be presented only as a synthesis of a datum yielded by the experiment with a possibility rejected in the experiment. He can know in a given case what the position (or velocity) *is* and what the velocity (or position) *might have been* (had it been measured instead); his actual knowledge of the particle is a combination of chosen and rejected possibilities or, in other words, of actuality and possibility.

Similarly, a theologian knows of the divine reality only by way of two different relations to it—the natural and the evangelical, or the atheistic and the theistic. He takes account of the yield of both relations, so that his question of deity in itself is like the theoretical question of what the particle is objectively. Abstractly the answer is: The "objective" reality is that which appears doubly (or "complementarily," to use Niels Bohr's word), depending on the subject or the measuring apparatus being used; and God is one who always *was* wrathful and threatening but who always *is* loving and saving, who always *was* nothing but always *will be* all in all. No whole view of reality is possible in any first-order relation, or literal experience; that we must look from one standpoint excludes our seeing from another. Depending on standpoint, any given deed may be seen either as an act of divine wrath or of divine love, nihilistic or wholly other in its depths. But if we take it in the one way, we cannot take the same deed in the other way. Only a second-order relation, that is to say, only a reflected relation is able to experience the phenomenon of God by way of the two first-order relations. Each standpoint on its own can be reflective in the sense of comparing the meaning of its assertions with an ascertainment of what is so; from each, one can experience the object and the truth of the object. But when we become aware of the standpoint as such, then we are referred for the whole truth to what is hidden in the various standpoints.

It should be noted that in neither of these two cases (physics, theology) do we have to do merely with differing points of view on an object which remains unaffected by the viewing. We cannot put the measurements of position and velocity of elementary particles nor the beliefs in nothing and God together as though they were points of view from which to see an unchanging reality. Theologians who think and speak of God as one who is both vengeful and forgiving and, dialectically, both nothing and wholly other, can do so only by a reflective ordering of the primary experiences of God as expressed in the natural and evangelical, the atheist and theist perceptions of what is so. Consequently, although one can form a composite image of a tree out of perceptions made from various points of view, one cannot form a composite experiment out of the two measurements of a particle or a composite symbol of God out of the two beliefs. The logic of God, like that of elementary particles, involves something other than a simple opposition between positive and negative. Atheism is not a simple negation of theism.

While the difference between standpoint and point of view should not be so emphasized as to becloud the similarities between them, it is important to keep this major difference in mind. Points of view are cumulative, standpoints are exclusive, in literal experience. In the reflective ordering of standpoints, therefore, there are two incompatible first-order subjects besides the reflective subject. The jeopardy, the "divided play," of theology originates in a difference of standpoint as well as a difference between reflection and primary experience; the question of truth brings both splits into view.

2

"God Is":
Meaning and Verification

A man is more likely to know what he is stating if it has been made clear how many meanings it may have.
— Aristotle, *Topics*, 108a, c.18

The meaning of the word "God" is determined . . . by the necessity of using the word "God."
— Gerhard Ebeling, *God and Word*, p. 33

As a matter of seeing the same in the different, the experience of truth embraces both meaning and reality; it has to do with "being," which appears in the assertion as meaning and in the projection and disclosure as reality. In Gerhard Ebeling's phrasing, "truth is reality set in words" (*G&W*, p. 23). So understood, being is the correlate of understanding rather than of perception or abstraction. As the division is commonly made, perception is of the singular, and abstract cognition is of the universal. Being, however, falls just between the two as the pure connection of singular to universal; it designates neither an individual nor a species or genus but an imperceptible and uncognizable connection of the two. It is "understood" but not "perceived" or "cognized." That is to say, one understands the "is" of a judgment and an entity, but one does not visualize it or define it. The act of understanding is, therefore, not to be confused with either the perception of singulars or the abstraction of universals.

To understand is to detect a sense in a sign. We understand the word "tree" if, for example, the word suggests an image of what

47

it designates. Being is a matter of understanding, rather than of perception, inasmuch as it is presented to us as a sense in a sign. This sign, however, is twofold. On the one hand, it is the set of words that comprise the proposition ("This is a tree") or, more restrictedly, the word "is" in that proposition. To understand the proposition is to see the sense in it, that is, to see being as meaning. But on the other hand, the sign is the appearing object itself; for to understand the object is to detect the connection between singular and universal (being as reality) that is signified by its very appearance to mind, an appearance that is expressed in the judgment.

Being becomes manifest in language, in the whole sense of a sentence. When a proposition is understood, being is opened to mind. The question of truth is whether how it manifests itself in meaning corresponds to how it manifests itself in reality.

But understanding can itself be made the correlate of thought; we can understand what it is that we understand. From this arise the discipline of interpretation and the theory of hermeneutics. They are based on the possibility of saying what has been understood through an act that is different from the original understanding of what is said and what is so. If one has understood what the sentence "The leaf is green" says, but when called upon to explain what has been understood, can only reply, "That the leaf is green," one understands the sentence without understanding what one has understood. The reply is not an interpretation. It becomes an interpretation when it is on this order: "I have understood the being, the essence, that appears in the object which I apprehend as a physical thing of a certain color, a green leaf." This may not be a sterling example, but it is an interpretation.

Interpretation and verification belong together insofar as being comprises both meaning and reality. If truth is the identity between being as a meaning understood and being as a reality disclosed, then determining whether a statement is true depends on interpreting what it means, at least in those cases where the meaning is obscure or multiple. To some extent hermeneutics and verification have been separated in the discussions over the last decades, and one of the results has been the failure, in discussions of the existence of God, to coordinate the verification with the several possible meanings of the assertion "God is"; there has been a corresponding failure in recent theologies to distinguish between interpreting doctrines or beliefs by means of philosophical systems (those of Marx, Bloch, Whitehead, and Habermas, to name some) and showing that the beliefs so understood are true. No doubt this development is partly due to the different origins of hermeneutics and verification-theory. The former is associated with phenomenological thought stemming from Heidegger and Husserl and, farther back, from Schleiermacher; the latter has been explored chiefly by analytical thought with its roots in the philosophy of science and in Hume and the Kant of the first two *Critiques*. Interpretation has to do with making clear the meaning of what is said; verification has to do with determining whether what is said is true. Since these do not seem to be one and the same undertaking, it is understandable that the two lines of development would be drawn independently of each other.

The separation needs to be counteracted, especially in respect to basic theological assertions, by a deliberate effort to interpret as well as to verify. This is not to say, of course, that every work must do both. There is a place for interpreting a tradition of doctrine according to current thought, particularly when the insistent question is not whether something is believed but what the belief amounts to or how what seems clearly to be so can be so. Still, to understand something is not the same as seeing its truth, and interpretation must at some time give way to verification.

On occasion it has been held that in religion interpretation and verification do amount to the same inasmuch as interpreting religious symbols and texts is the manner of verifying them. Three varieties of this position can be sketched here so as to indicate the reasons for taking it as well as the reasons why it seems untenable except in a limited way. It appears in a phenomenological dress in Paul Tillich of the 1920s, in a metaphysical one in Charles Hartshorne, and in a hermeneutical one in certain tendencies in the hermeneutical discussion.

In his early work on the philosopy of religion Tillich advanced the view that in religious assertions the question of meaning is the same as that of truth: "The question of the truth of religion is answered by metalogically grasping the essence of religion as directedness toward the unconditional meaning. It makes no sense to ask in addition whether the unconditional 'exists [*ist*],' that is, whether the religious act is directed to something real and to that extent is true or false" ("Religionsphilosophie," p. 327). What is grasped in a religious assertion is unconditional meaning, and it lies in the nature of the unconditional to be presupposed even by the doubt about it. To ask whether an expression of unconditional meaning is true is to have failed to understand the unconditional meaning. If the question of truth is raised about a religious assertion, it can be answered only by an interpretation of the assertion which brings out its unconditional meaning. The question is a symptom of misunderstanding.[1]

Hartshorne's conception of the way metaphysical questions and the "central religious question" (*AD*, p. 24) are "self-answering" has the same result. "Anselm's discovery," he writes, "amounts to this: there are persons who believe in the divine existence, and these, if they understand their faith, are *the only ones who understand it;* the others, whether they are believers lacking understanding or 'unbelievers,' are all people who do not clearly know the meaning of 'belief in God' " (p. 97). The question of God's existence is a self-answering metaphysical one. Although it does involve a matter of fact and not merely of formal definition, its answer is provided as soon as the idea contained in it is correctly understood. Experience can neither confirm nor refute it. But as soon as one becomes clear on what the idea of God as the one "surpassable only by himself"—Hartshorne's reformulation of Anselm's *id quo majus cogitari nequit*, "that than which no greater can be thought"—entails, one knows that God exists because it is self-contradictory to assert that he does not. There may indeed be someone greater than God at any stated moment, but this greater one is God himself at a future moment.

The burden of this contention is the same as in Anselm—one cannot both rightly understand what is meant by "God" and also deny that he exists. A demonstration of divine existence, or a verification of the assertion that God exists, is provided by making clear what the idea of God really means; when such an interpretation is provided, the question answers itself. Despite its argumentative form, the aim of the demonstration is to bring about a recognition of what is implicit in the meaning of the idea of God. That this aim is carried out in Hartshorne's case within a metaphysical rather than a hermeneutical setting is indicated by its resting on the law of contradiction as an inviolable negative criterion for what is thought and what is so. Admittedly, the vulnerability of any metaphysical argument is to be found in just this use of the law of contradiction; for if it is not self-contradictory to think that internally contradictory ideas may correspond to realities, then the possibility of metaphysics needs first to be demonstrated. This matter aside, however, the notion that the existence of God is a self-answering question exemplifies the position that interpretation and verification come to the same thing—to understand what is meant by an assertion is to see that and how it is true, and atheism is accordingly a matter of misunderstanding what theism is saying.

A third variation on this position derives from a theological adaptation of truth as *aletheia.* It is characteristic not so much of a particular representative as of a tendency pervading contemporary hermeneutics. According to this view, an interpreter of historic texts does not ask merely what a text means, nor does he ask whether what it says is true; rather, he asks *what* its truth is, or more exactly, he "resays" it so that its truth appears. The criterion of interpretation is the extent to which the truth expressed by a text is indeed brought to light, either by an explanation which lets the original words speak again or by putting the same truth into new words that speak it effectively. A New Testament parable, for example is read not only with a view to understanding what the author or authors had in mind but also with the aim of retelling the story so that the hearers of the parable recognize it as true of them. It is not quite accurate to say—in a variation of Ebeling's wording in another context (*WuG*, I, p. 198)—that the text verifies the hearer rather than the other way around. A hearer does verify the text, he does see that it is true; but he sees it as true of himself. Indeed, retelling a parable has truth in view both as manifestation and as correspondence. It seeks to open the hearer's eyes so that he sees something about himself that he did not see before and so that he sees it as corresponding to who he really is. Even if the truth is recognizable only inwardly by a hearer about himself, it is still a matter of a correspondence between what is told of him and what is so about him.

To verify is, etymologically, to "make true." Ebeling uses this sense in order to distinguish two ways of putting the question of verification. It is one thing to ask how that of which theology speaks can be verified as reality; it is another thing to ask how that of which theology speaks verifies reality (*WuG*, I, p. 198). The former question, Ebeling argues, is still under the spell of an epistemology that is oriented to the standpoint of perception and observation (*betrachtendes Wahrnehmen*). Applying Ebeling's distinction to a New Testament parable will illustrate what is implied. If a parable speaks of the kingdom of God, the question of theological verification is not whether we can observe the kingdom of God to see whether it is in reality like what the parable shows. Instead, the question is whether the kindgom of God, which "is like" the happening the parable narrates, accords with the reality in which we live by making it true. The function of the parable is to show this reality, with which we are already acquainted, in another way so as to bring out a truth about it that had not been seen. Where a hearer can say in response to the parable, "Yes, that is how things are," he has understood it.

Speaking of the kingdom of God—or, generally, that of which theology speaks—invites another procedure of verification than the one employed in speaking of the American nation. "The

American nation is like a drunken giant" is a metaphorical expression that in principle is verifiable by how the nation is operating. If the assertion is true, then it is so because that is how the American democracy in reality is. The kingdom of God, however, does not name any special entity, as does "the American nation"; and the question of whether what is said about it is true has to do with whether what is said of the kingdom of God makes it possible to understand everyday reality in a new way. This is a matter of whether speaking of the kingdom of God has the capacity to show things so that we can see them in that way, i.e., as the kingdom of God. Theological assertions are true when they enable hearers or readers to see things in the way that they are set forth in those assertions.

In one procedure of verification, *reality* (what is so) "makes true," or *verifies, an assertion* because how it shows itself corresponds to what was said about it. Heidegger's phrasing for this is that the thing shows itself to be in itself the same as it was in the assertion. In the other procedure, an *assertion verifies the reality* to which it refers because what it says about the reality corresponds to how the reality shows itself in the light of that assertion. But the contrast is not so sharp as Ebeling's wording seems to make it; furthermore, it is not strictly so that that about which theology speaks (God) verifies reality. What is meant by "reality" is, after all, that about which the assertion speaks. The contrast between two procedures, however, is worth noting. To ask whether what is so can be verified by what we say about it is different from asking whether what we say is verified by what is so. In both cases the truth has to do with the correspondence of the one to the other. But to ask "Is it true that the leaf is green?" is to inquire whether the leaf is green, whereas to ask "What words express what the green leaf is, i.e., what it means for the leaf to be the thing it is?" is to inquire what words will say, or bring to light, the sense of the leaf's being what it is.

That this conception of hermeneutics nevertheless tends to conflate understanding a text with the ascertainment of whether what it says is true is shown by how it presupposes the truth. An axiom is that a text has not been correctly interpreted until its truth has been brought out (in a way similar to what happens in the successful retelling of a parable). The essential meaning of a biblical text is said not be be understood at all if the hearer does not recognize it as true about himself. The origin of this axiom is the Protestant doctrine of the Scriptures as the word of God. But it has a general application too. There is no such thing as a text whose meaning may be understood but which may be judged to be false. In circumstances where that seems to be the case— where a hearer or reader believes he has understood the text but ascertains that what it says does not agree with how things are— hermeneutical theory views the text as not yet understood in its own meaning.

One should not, however, confuse this implicit axiom in hermeneutical practice with what R. M. Háre set forth as the incorrigibility of "bliks"—views of reality held so tenaciously that all occurrences are interpreted as confirming them. One of Hare's illustrations is that of a college student who thinks all dons are plotting against him. If they exhibit anger toward him, this is confirmation of his "blik"; if they exhibit friendliness, this too confirms the "blik" because it is interpreted as only a devious way for the dons to carry out their plot. If anything and everything is to be seen as the working of the kingdom of God, this seems to be similar to the working of a "blik." Everything confirms, and nothing refutes, what a parable tells.

Yet there is an important difference. For the issue in interpretation is one of letting the text itself show things in a certain way. The starting point is not that the hearer or reader has a view of things which he sees confirmed by everything that happens. Rather, the starting point is that the hearer does not see things as they are presented in the parable, and the truth of the parable lies just in its power to change the view of things that he already has. If people have "bliks" of the sort Hare describes, then what the parable does is just the opposite of what occurrences in the world do—it counteracts the "blik." The parable can be repeatedly verified by whether, every time the "blik"-holder with his interpretation of everything is presented with the parable by being told it or retold it, he is enabled to see things not according to his "blik" but according to how the parable shows them. What prevents the parable of the kingdom of God from becoming a "blik" itself is that its subject-matter is the kingdom of God, that is, *not* the world of everyday experience. If the truth of the parable is experienced, then the hearer of the parable is enabled to see that how things actually show themselves in a light true to them corresponds to how the parable shows them. But which light—that of common language or that of theology—is true to them? On this last matter hermeneutical theory usually falters.

All three variations on the idea that meaning and truth are the same in religion invite suspicion for the same reason—they deny that truth can be experienced as such. The problem lies not so much in what they do as in what they do not do. They have their own validity, but they need to be joined with something else to overcome the suspicion. Standing alone they not only seem to exempt theological assertions from the critical control maintained over assertions, they also seem to eradicate an essential aspect of the difference in the identity of meaning and reality. If no difference can be seen between the meaning that is understood in the words and the reality that is disclosed in the object, then it is not possible to see identity in difference; truth cannot be experienced. In other cases it is possible to understand meanings carried by the signs and to recognize that the meaning understood is that of the signs (although mistakes can be made) without knowing whether the meaning accords with the reality it signifies. Seeing that it is true does not mean understanding a meaning but seeing that this meaning as understood does accord with how things are.

Furthermore, the openness of this experience implies that how one now sees things may be corrected by future ascertainments. The quest for "absolute truth" may lead us to expect a point at which perfect identity overcomes all difference. But from the foregoing analysis such an expectation must be regarded—to put it ironically—as untruthful. As Michael

Theunissen remarked in a study of truth in Hegel, the drive implicit in truth as correspondence may be toward unity, so that unity (*Einheit*) is expected in the end to replace correspondence (*Entsprechung*) in constituting absolute truth; but at the point where that occurs, truth also vanishes. "Perfect ... correspondence ... is at the same time *no* correspondence" ("Begriff," p. 194).

Every ascertainment can become the starting concept for a further verification when doubt arises. Thus the contention that meaning and truth come to the same seems to confuse a starting situation with the reflective situation in which truth can be experienced. At the start when, in view of an object, one asserts that the thing there is a tree, what is meant and what is seen to be so do agree with each other. But it may turn out that the perception of the object was wrong because the distance was too great or the lighting poor or there was some other hindrance. When that happens, one does not say that a second person, who finds the assertion to be false, has failed to understand what was said; instead, an effort is made to determine who is in error. To hold that an assertion can be regarded as false only until its meaning is understood seems to be possible only in the limited sense that every assertion does give expression to an actual (though perhaps mistaken) perception of an object as it was thought to be, or in the subjective sense that every assertion may truly express a belief or an intention to deceive on the part of the one who made it even when the belief does not accord with fact or the intention is defeated.

In sum, although unclear theological assertions need to be interpreted before they can be verified, interpretation is not the same as verification. There are interpretive questions involved in the theological assertion "God is." But it is possible to understand rightly what the assertion says without yet knowing whether what it asserts is true. At issue, therefore, is the twofold question of what those words mean and whether they are true. In the present chapter the exposition will be directed to the meaning and the manner of verification; the next chapter will consider to what extent truth is experienced in the assertion according to its various meanings. The criterion resulting from an analysis of reflective experience is that we can see the truth of assertions just to the extent that both the difference and the identity are maintained.

The Senses of "God Is"

The meaning of "God is" is unclear, partly because all theological language seems foreign in a language shaped by criticism and secular concern, and partly because, even when intelligible, the assertion has multiple meanings. A "text" like "God is" requires a translation as well as an interpretation. Although the two are not entirely different undertakings, translation is needed when words cannot be understood at all and must be replaced by understandable ones, and interpretation is needed when several meanings can be understood in the words, or there is a hidden meaning, and when other words do not replace them but are correlated with them. The criterion for a transposition which is both a translation and an interpretation is whether in the process the unintelligible sounds become intelligible and can be correlated with, but not replaced by, the other intelligible ones. The distinction should not be belabored, but the account which follows has the character partly of a translation and partly of an interpretation.

"God is" is open to three distinct readings. It can be taken as equivalent to "God exists," which in turn is equivalent to "There is someone or something that is God." In such a case it asserts that there is an entity that possesses the properties designated by the name "God." This is the reading almost always taken in discussions of the proofs for God's existence. "If, now, we say 'God is,' or 'There is a God,' we attach no new predicate to the concept of God, but only posit the subject in itself . . . and . . . as an object that stands in relation to my concept," Kant wrote (*CrPuR*, A599/B627, p. 505). " 'God exists' must mean," Gilbert Ryle concluded, "what is meant by 'Something, and one thing only, is omniscient, omnipotent, and infinitely good (or whatever else are the characters summed up in being the compound character of being a God and the only God)" (Ramsey, *Words*, p. 130). That this is a possible interpretation of "God is" can scarcely be denied. But it is not the only one; and since the other readings tend to be lost to view, they need to be elaborated somewhat more.

A second reading, one suggested by Anselm's comparison of the relation among essence, *esse*, and existence to that of *lux*, *lucere*, and *lucens* understands "God is" to involve the ascription of the action of being to an agent whose essential act is to be. As "shining" (*lucere*) is what light (*lux*) does just by virtue of its being light, so "being" (*esse*) is what God does just by virtue of his being God. On this reading "God is" has the same kind of validity that "light shines (*lux lucet*)" has, and hence Aquinas can remark that the "most appropriate" name for God is not *Deus*, which is based on the "universal providence" of the divine—a comment recalling the probable origin of *Deus* in the Greek word *theasthai*—but *qui est*, the one who is. "To be" is what God, as God, does. Light cannot but *lucere*, and God cannot but *esse*.

Third, "God is" may be understood as asserting that God is someone without specifying more exactly who or what he is. On this reading "God is" is an incomplete assertion waiting to be filled out by another word: "God is *G*." However similar in meaning "*G* is God" (the first reading, discussed earlier) and "God is *G*" (the present reading) might appear to be at the outset, there is a fundamental difference between them which warrants treating "God is *G*" as a distinct meaning not to be reduced to the first one.

The difference between the two can be seen in an everyday example. It is one thing to say "This is a tree"; it is another thing to say "A tree is this." In both cases "this" points out a thing in view or in mind. But in the former case a perceptible object is named, while in the latter a term is ostensively defined. The former fits a name with a thing; the latter fits a thing with a name. The latter, ostensive assertion indicates in what thing a term is exemplified or shown. Having read a dictionary definition or heard a word used, one may ask what that word means.

The question is answered not by a further definition of the term but by pointing out objects—"A tree is: this, and this, and this . . ." Such ostensive definitions do not tell us what an object is, but they point out where to look in order to see how, or as what, the object is what it is. In the same fashion "God is" can be understood as the beginning of an assertion answering the question of where that which is meant by the word "God" is to be perceived.

An example of such a usage may be seen in Euripides' *Helen*. Upon recognizing her husband Menelaus, Helen exclaims, "Gods! For god [is] even the recognition of dear ones." The beginning of the Gospel of John (John 1:1) may provide a second example in "God was—the word." Of course, the English translation, "The word was God," is technically correct according to the rule of Greek grammar that in an identical proposition the subject is the noun with the definite article and the predicate is the noun without article, regardless of the position of the two nouns. Peter Hodgson seems to overlook this rule when he remarks that "the word order suggests that the translation" of the passage should be "God was the word" rather than "The word was God" ("Heidegger," p. 248). Nevertheless Hodgson's point may be correct. The grammatical rule is formulated without regard to the difference between a judgment, in which the predicate delimits the subject, and an ostensive assertion, in which the predicate term cites the appearing of the subject.

But we do not need to go back to ancient Greek for examples. Some of Hartshorne's statements about the distinction between the "existence" and the "actuality" of God run in the same direction. He thus concludes that the ontological argument provides a proof to the effect that God is actualized somehow (that is his "bare existence") but that it does not give any indication about the way in which God is actualized. That is to say, what we can at all events know is that God is not nothing, he is someone or something. We can know this in advance and on the basis of the idea of God as the one who is not surpassable by another. But where and how he is actualized, or how he actually is the unsurpassable one, is a matter of investigation. This interpretation gives to "God is" a sense distinct from "There is someone or something that is God."

On this reading of "God is," as we shall see, the truth of "God is *G*" (where *G* means some actuality) does not imply the truth of "*G* is God." Accordingly, "God is Jesus of Nazareth" could be true and "Jesus of Nazareth is God" false, or conversely; for the former assertion states where the one named God makes an appearance, and the latter defines what or who Jesus is.

In principle this reading of "God is" breaks with the alternative set for Greek metaphysics by Parmenides' dictum "Being is and nonbeing is not." If the two axioms which constitute that metaphysics are those two tautologies, then "God is *G*," which is to say "God is not-nothing," breaks out of the metaphysical system. It fits with neither of the axioms; for God is neither entity that is, nor nonentity that is not. Rather, God appears just between being and nonbeing, and the name "God" signifies one that belongs nowhere in the metaphysical alternative because it is the excluded third possibility, the *tertium* of the *tertium non datur*. This applies even to the Kantian understanding of being as equivalent to objectivity. If "being is being" is recast as "objectivity is objectivity" and "nonbeing is not" is recast as "subjectivity is subjectivity," then "God" is (in Schelling's phrase) subject-object, or the source and identity of objectivity and subjectivity; he is not a subject in opposition to an object nor an object in opposition to a subject but a subjective-objective unity which, as soon as it becomes objective for a subject, loses its deity. But to "be" such a subject-object is neither the being of "being is" nor the nothing of "nonbeing is not." The double negative of "God is not-nothing" is not the same as the positive of "God is being."

Verification According to the Three Readings
1. "God Exists"
It is clear that the three meanings of "God is" are affected by the question of truth in different ways. "God exists" is true to the

extent that there is someone or something that possesses divine attributes. The claim to truth for this assertion must be justified by showing that there is an entity that can rightly be called and be known to be God, and the truth of the assertion lies in a correspondence between what the words "This one is God" are understood to say and what is ascertained to be so about the one they signify. The ascertainment of what is so may be made *inferentially*, if we can show that what we know to be so about other things leads to the conclusion that there is a God; or it may be undertaken *experientially*, if we can demonstrate that some object of experience possesses divine attributes. The various proofs of the existence of God drawn from the nature of the world or of human being, the cosmological and moral arguments, belong to the former kind of undertaking; accounts of religious experience generally belong to the latter insofar as they deal with the overwhelming element in such experience.

Wilhelm Herrmann's influential philosophy of religion, of which there are many traces in Barth as well as in Bultmann and with which Tillich explicitly debated in his early theses on christology (1911), occupies a ground between these two positions. His demonstration is experiential and inferential at the same time. It can be summarized in three points: 1) that God exists means that there is a power, greater than all things, in whom we can place trust unreservedly; 2) the "picture of Jesus" presented in the New Testament is experienced in such a way that the "total picture of Jesus' inner life . . . compels us to simple reverence" (*Communion*, p. 75): it makes such an impression on us that we cannot doubt the reality of the event; 3) we find it impossible to attribute this experience to any other source than God: "The man who has felt these simple experiences [viz., the "sense of condemnation" and the "startled sense" felt at the "disclosure of actual living goodness in his person"] cannot possibly attribute them to any other source. The God in whom he now believes for Jesus' sake is as real and living to him as the man Jesus in his marvelous sublimity of character" (p. 98). The "existence of Jesus in this world of ours" is "the fact in which God so touches

us as to come into a communion with us that can endure" (p. 98).
The reason why the "fact of Jesus' inner life" can establish the
"certainty of God that is superior to every doubt" (p. 97) is that
the idea implied in our unconditional confidence, which is awakened by the picture of Jesus—"the idea of a Power . . . which will
see to it that Jesus . . . , who lost his life in this world, will be
nonetheless victorious over the world" (p. 96)—takes hold of us
on its own as much as does the impression of the person of Jesus.
"Thus God makes himself known to us as the Power that is with
Jesus in such a way that amid all our distractions and the mist of
doubt He can never again entirely vanish from us" (p. 98).

There are echoes of Herrmann, as well as a critique of this
argument, when Barth, in the section on "God is" (*KD*, II/1, §28),
repeatedly reminds readers that what is of theological concern is
not the impressiveness of an experience—not even if it is the
experience of redemption—but whether the occurrence, or any
other one, be it ever so unimpressive, is a deed of *God*. "*God* and
not being—being only as the being of *God* is our object" (*KD*, I/1,
p. 292). And Tillich's theses on christology argue that Herrmann
in effect bases the knowledge of God upon the experience of the
picture of Jesus as a kind of inference from this picture. This
refutation, it must be admitted, overlooks a nuance in
Herrmann's thought; for Herrmann emphasizes that the
"thought of such a power," that is, the thought of God, and the
"impression of the person of Jesus" both "lay hold" of us—it is
not a matter of inferring the one from the other.

Such efforts to ascertain whether someone or something is
God are, however, dubious for two reasons. In the first place,
religious consciousness finds the very effort self-defeating. Religion does not regard God as one to be judged by an available
criterion. To say "This must have been the working of God because no one else could have done it" is to imply that one has a
criterion by which to decide what is godly and what is not. But to
employ a criterion in order to judge whether there is a deity
behind the appearances of the world or whether a certain experience is an experience of the living God is to elevate the

criterion itself to supreme status. What we ascertain to meet certain standards cannot in truth be the deity because it is subject to something else, a criterion by which it is judged.

To avoid this result, an ascertainment that something is God would have to be made in such a way that the criterion used in making the ascertainment is shown to be identical with the appearance of the object that it judges, and Herrmann seems to intend something on this order by having the criterion (the thought of God) come from the object of the experience (the impression of the picture of Jesus), so that the figure of Jesus which is the datum of reality is also what makes it "impossible" for us to ascribe that "fact in our lives" to anyone but God. But if this is taken strictly, then we are not really ascertaining, but only repeating, that something said to be God is God.

From an endeavor to show that Jesus is God one of two things must result. Either the criterion used to judge that Jesus is God is other than the appearance of Jesus himself, in which case it is not Jesus but the criterion that is in fact God since Jesus is subject to it. Or the criterion used to judge that Jesus is God is identical with the appearance of Jesus; but then no line can be drawn between how he appears and how he is, and consequently the ascertainment is not really an ascertainment of reality but a repetition of the concept. There is an identity without a difference. To reply that the deity has given the human mind a criterion by which to recognize it only defers the matter to another question; namely, "Is it true that such a criterion has been so given?" Similarly, if the reply is that a criterion which is the greatest in the order of cognition is not the greatest in the order of reality (a distinction that Aquinas appeals to), the matter is only displaced for the time being. It reemerges in the question of what the order of cognition "really is" in relation to the order of reality.

In the second place, the undeniable circumstance that no inferential or experiential proof has yet been devised that convinces everyone capable of following the proof must indicate there is something amiss in appealing to canons of thought or to experience for a proof that some entity is divine.

These objections could be met, theoretically, if an argument (or an ascertainment) were constituted by two distinct steps, one in which a criterion is applied in order to show that an appearance in question is indeed God because it possesses the attributes of God, and a second step in which it is shown that the criterion thus applied is not itself a judge over the appearance. The act of ascertaining that someone is God must be at the same time an act in which it is not only we who make the ascertainment but also God who, in our act, makes the ascertainment about himself. This is to say that in one respect (that is, as a criterion which we understand and have at our disposal) the critierion is a judge of anything that appears as God and thus is *not* the same as the object it judges, and that in another respect or, more exactly, in another moment of the demonstration the criterion *is* the same as the objective appearance it judges because it discloses itself as the agent of our own act of judging. To show how this can be done was the aim of the speculative idealist "theological"—as against the "reflective"—demonstration of God. In the theological proof it is not only the theologian who demonstrates the existence of God but God who, in the demonstration, demonstrates himself. But the difficulty of executing such a proof, instead of merely projecting it, is very great indeed; one is put on guard when Daub, one of its representatives, warns that the demonstration is carried out only in the whole course of the dogmatic system.

2. "Who Is, Is"

If "God is" is understood not as equivalent to the assertion that there is someone that is God ("God exists") but, instead, as ascribing an act to an agent, then its truth or falsehood does not depend upon there being or not being someone of whom it can be ascertained that he possesses divine properties. Experiencing the truth of the assertion is not dependent upon seeing a correspondence between what the assertion says and what is ascertained to be so. It depends, rather, on whether the one in the many is made manifest.

Consider again the relation between *lux* and *lucere*. Is it true that *lux lucet?* Of course, it is, for "shine" is the word used in order to designate that appearance by virtue of which something is called a light. By denomination, what shines is light; and any particular thing, such as a lamp, capable of shining can be—to make a play on words—an "illustration" of light.

Since shining is not a property a thing possesses but an action a thing performs, the predicate term in "This is a light" is of another order than in "This is a tree." "Tree" designates a generic concept. "Light" names an agent, a source of the process "shining"; it does not define what a lamp, a fire, and a bulb are, nor does it cite a property with respect to which lamps, fires, and bulbs exhibit specific differences. Strictly speaking, then, a light cannot "exist" as does a tree, or a lamp, a bulb, and a fire. The reason is important, although it is easily overlooked. To say that something is a light is not to assert that it is a thing-there possessing certain properties associated with a generic or specific concept but to name the subject of a perceived action or process.

Accordingly, if "is" (*est*) is to "God" (*qui est*) as "shines" (*lucet*) is to "light" (*lux*), then what bears on the truth of "God is" is not the existence but the be-ing of an entity. Any entity, to the extent that it "is," bears the same relation to God as a particular light-source bears to *lux*; as it is light which by name is the subject shining in all particular shinings, so it is God who "is" in the be-ing of all entities.

In this reading, the "God" of "God is" designates the agent of action in the same way that "walker" designates the agent of walking. The one who "is walking" is always a "walker," just as the one that is shining ("lighting") is always a light. In the same way, the one that is is always "God" inasmuch as the word "God" means nothing other than the "be-er," the agent of the action of being. We could not imagine perceiving an action of "is-walking" without simultaneously perceiving the one who is walking; what we see is never just "walking" but rather that someone is walking, or the walking of someone; this one is at all events the walker of that walking.

There is a difference, then, between asserting that a walker is walking (or a light is shining) and asserting that Socrates is walking or that a bulb is shining. In the latter cases we have to do with an object that is perceptible and definable apart from the action of which it is said to be the agent. In interpreting "God is," one must be careful to maintain initially that "God " is definable and perceivable in no other way than as the agent of the act of being. The sense of "God is" is simply this that "the 'be-er' (*qui est*) is." When it is asked, "Who is walking there?" the obvious answer is "A walker." To identify that "walker" with an entity otherwise known and definable requires an additional step.

This additional step has to do with whether "God *is* the 'be-er,' " that is to say, (1) whether "is" makes manifest the underlying action for all actions and events, so that whatever is going on and being done can be seen as a matter of be-ing and (2) whether "God" makes manifest the underlying agent of everything that occurs. The content of the assertion is that if anything is anything at all, and if anything occurs or is done, then "God is," in the same way that if any bulb or fire or lamp is shining, then "light is shining."

That the one agent and action do not exist in the same manner as do the many is illustrated by Ryle's frequently cited example of a category mistake. The "university," he wrote, is not "an extra member" of the class to which the libraries and the colleges belong (Ramsey, *Words*, p. 135). Thus, for a foreigner to say "I have seen the colleges and the rest, but where is Oxford university?" is to betray a misunderstanding of what the word "university" signifies. Similarly, with respect to this second reading of "God is," to say "I have seen people walking and heard them talking and watched plants growing, but where do I find God be-ing?" is like asking where the university of Oxford is among the colleges, libraries, administrative offices, and the rest. "God" is the category of someone as such, the agent as such, which is the origin of action. To ask whether, alongside such events as those designated by "It is raining," "I am talking," "N is walking," there is

another one, "God is be-ing," is to confuse the categories. To
recognize this, of course, is not the same as determining how we
come to know the content of the unique category, the one in the
many, nor does it clarify what the difference and identity are (the
difference which Heidegger referred to as the unthought difference between the one who is and anyone who is), nor, finally,
does it preclude the possibility that this unique one in the many
can also appear as one among the many.

Speculative idealism proposed that the role of the proofs of
the existence of God is really that of elevating the consciousness
so that thinking becomes aware of the one in the many. Thus, for
Schelling the proof that "God is" consists in nothing else, and
nothing less, than a disclosure of the necessary "act" of saying or
thinking the absolute in all events. The starting point is that the
consciousness of objects as independent of consciousness, that is,
objects which are just there as resistances in the way without a
sense or meaning, is negated by the idea of truth, by the notion
that it is possible to put such objects into words. This negation
leads to the replacement of the manifold world of sensation with
the idea of unity and identity. To carry out this movement is not
a matter of constructing an argument for the existence of an
absolute on the basis of the finite world, but it is a matter of
annulling, or seeing through, the reality of finite things. The
absolute is reached by liberating the subject inwardly from the
contingent, and by its becoming one with the essential identity.
This is not a formal deduction; it is an act, but an act which the
idea of truth makes necessary and an act in which freedom is
absorbed in the necessity (Tillich, *Mysticism*, p. 100).

Similarly, the dialectical *Erhebung* of consciousness in Hegel's
phenomenology is an ascent from everyday consciousness, which
is aware only of the difference and opposition between the self
and its object, to an absolute consciousness, aware of the oneness
of spirit acting in the particular subjectivity of finite spirit. "The
opposition between objectivity and subjectivity is in itself overcome," Hegel wrote; "our task is to make ourselves participants

of this redemption by letting go of our immediate subjectivity and becoming conscious of God as our true and essential self" (Schweitzer, "Geist," p. 325).

The task with which this assertion of "God is" thus presents us is not that of determining whether there is something that has such properties as preeminent justice and infinite love, but that of penetrating the particular agents and actions so as to see and to show the one agent which is be-ing in all events. But the experience of truth has to do with identity in difference, first of all between meaning and reality. Thus a question arises concerning what here are the identity and the difference. If "God" is nothing but a stipulated sign for the one agent and "is" is nothing but a like sign for the one action, then the truth of "God is" is a matter not of experience but of formal stipulation. One could as well use any other signs for the three letters of "God" and the two letters of "is." To assert, however, that "God is" is true implies that the words are not merely designations of an underlying one but that they manifest such a one as other than a formal unification of events and deeds and also as other than the particular subjects who too "are" something.

Two matters of difference are, accordingly, involved. First, the circumstance that "God is" is not just a formal sign but also other than the sign, the one to which the sign points and which it states, is the difference manifested by the power of language, which impels us to use the words "God is" and not some other combination of letters. Second, there is a difference between the one and the many—the one subject, or agent, of all actions differs from the many subjects, and the one action of be-ing differs from the many actions through which it is concretely manifested. To say that N is running is not equivalent to saying that God is be-ing. N is not God, and be-ing is not running. Yet there is an identity in this difference which, like the sameness between the meaning of an assertion and the ascertainment of a fact, makes a correspondence possible. A concept is not a reality, and a reality is not a concept; yet what is said and what is so are the same, and the "is" of the proposition is the same as the "is" of the reality. Similarly, God is not N and N is not God; yet when N is running this is the same as when God is be-ing.

The shift of categories, as indicated by how the sameness is formulated, is to be noted. *What* is said in an assertion is the same as what is so in the self-presentation of an object; but *when* God is be-ing is the same as when something else is taking place. The experience of truth occurs with respect to an objective assertion when the same content is seen in the meaning and in the reality, which as such are different from each other. With respect to the manifestation of the one in the many, this experience is to see that there is a sameness in the difference between the one agent and action and the many concrete agents and actions. This latter mode of the experience differs from the former in that time enters into it differently. The difference between meaning and reality is a difference in time; a reality shows that it "is" the entity that "was" meant in the assertion. *What* is said and what is so are the same; the same words can be used to project the reality and to register its appearance. But *when* it is said and when it is so are different. By contrast, *when* God is is the same as when N is running, whereas who or *what* God is is different from who or what N is. In experiencing the truth of other assertions we have to do with the identity of the "what" in the difference between saying and being, whereas in the truth of manifestations (as in "God is") we have to do with the identity of the "when" in the difference between the one and the many. The first is the *identity of substance in the difference in time*; the second is the *identity of time in the difference of subjects or events*.

The nature of this difference can perhaps be made clearer by reference to how language is involved. The mark of truth in an assertion (e.g., "The painting on the wall is crooked") is that the same words can be used to express both the meaning (when we have our back toward the wall) and the reality (how the painting shows itself, or appears, when we turn around). To the extent that the wording which projects the referent, and the wording which ascertains how the referent appears, are one and the same, the assertion is true; the words which say, and the words which show, what something is are identical.

In the truth that is the identity in difference between the one and the many, the matter is otherwise. Here we have to do with two wordings that apply to one referent, both as that referent is projected in the saying and as it is shown in the ascertaining. About one and the same objective occurrence it can be said, "N runs" and "God is"; the two wordings both project the event and ascertain it. To see the sameness in difference, accordingly, is to see that "N runs" and "God is" say a different meaning and show a different reality and yet the time of both meanings and both realities is the same; it is to see that the time which is said by the language and shown by the reality of the many subjects and their many actions is the same as the time which is said by the language and shown by the reality of the one subject (God) and the one action (be-ing).

This experience is made possible when something in the meaning of an assertion ("N runs") suggests, or brings to light, a second meaning ("God is"), which is in and with the first one; and, corresponding to it, something in the reality (N's running) signifies a second reality (God's being) that is in and with the literal one. In Hartshorne's thought it is the idea of greatness that performs this function; in Schelling it is the idea of truth. Aquinas makes use of the idea of comparison in the fourth *via* for demonstrating that God is—the notion of an attribute has within it not only the literal meaning but also the capacity to point to a second meaning, and this capacity is the element of comparability or degree.

In reference to the one in the many, however, it is more exactly the duplicity of the word "one"—which can mean "singular" as well as "only"—that performs this function. "N runs" bespeaks that one is running; but the "one" of "one is running" has in it the double sense of "someone, anyone" and of "one and no other." This double sense provides the power by which a meaning signifies a second meaning and a reality conveys a second reality. The duplicity appears to arise from the formation of language rather than from that of ideas. It is exemplified not only by the word "one" but also by the word "nothing" in such phrasings as "He said nothing" (which can mean either that he did not speak at all or that he spoke but what he said was nugatory). But whatever be the source of its possibility, this phase of experiencing truth is a matter of seeing the correspondence between when God is be-ing and when anything else takes place, the correspondence between the occurring of the many and the be-ing of the one. The "when" of the one is the same as the "when" of the other. This presupposes, however, that time (the "when") is subject to modifications just as is the "what" of assertions. *What* is said is infinitely diverse; *when* something is said is also infinitely diverse. But the correspondence that is concretely the experience of truth is that of the "what" to the "what" or the "when" to the "when."

"God is," as a language which bespeaks the unity of events, may appear today as a foreign language. Even after it has been explained, one needs time (the phrasing is deliberate) before being able to hear its meaning, just as a native English speaker requires time before actually hearing meanings in the sounds of French words. The contemporary mentality finds it relatively easy to understand predications on the order of "This is a tree" and "A tree is a woody perennial plant having a single main stem, etc.," where the predicate term supplies a class or a definition to which the subject term can be assigned. But the same mentality is puzzled by predications in which the more universal term is not a generic property but a unity of events. For that reason "God is" in the second sense being discussed here poses a problem of understanding as well as of verification; it is an obscure text requiring interpretation before it can be verified, and it requires time before one actually understands it in this sense.

A suggestion from Hans-Georg Gadamer's hermeneutics may, however, offer assistance in understanding how we experience such unities; for by basing hermeneutics on the experience of play and of a work of art, Gadamer provides an access to what is meant by a language in which one speaks of the one subject and action underlying the many. Gadamer's theme is that "what meets us in the experience of the beautiful and in the understanding of the meaning of a tradition does actually have something of the truth of play" in it. But it is of the essence of a game or play that the "behavior of the player should not be understood as the behavior of a separate subject, since it is, rather, the play itself which does the playing by drawing the players into itself and which thus becomes the real subject of the movement of the play" (*WuM*, p. 464). So too "the 'subject' of the experience of art . . . is not the subjectivity of the one who experiences it, but the work of art itself" (p. 98). Similarly, the process of language is a play "of language itself, which addresses us, makes suggestions and withdraws them, questions and fulfills itself in the answer" (p. 465). Such a hermeneutical theory makes clear how particular subjects (players) are related to an underlying subject (the game) by being drawn into it; in so doing the theory prepares the ground for taking the further step of showing how all events are related to the one underlying event "God is."

What we experience while playing a game or while being caught up in it as spectators is that there are two different orders of agent at work. The one order is composed of the players themselves. Each has a particular role to play in relation to the others. Each is a subject of his own movements, an agent of his own actions. Thus, to a question of who scored a point during a game, the answer can be given with the name of one of the players. But in addition to these players a subject of another order is at work, the game itself. Players determine their actions not only by the actions of other players but also by the rules of the game. These rules are, of course, not the same thing as the game. But they are the formal regulations which make it possible for the game they define to be played at all and to present itself through the playing. The game presents itself when the rules are put into play. This is its *Selbstdarstellung*.

Accordingly, the game is, on the one hand, what the players

play. But on the other hand, it is what presents itself through their playing. They do not present it in the way that, for example, one presents a gift to someone, but it presents itself through their playing of it. The real game cannot be separated from the playing of it; for only in the playing is it represented for what it is.

That the game is a subject on its own, manifest in and yet distinct from the individual subjects who are the players, is indicated by the power of the game to draw one into it—regardless of whether one is a player or a spectator—and by the respect that the rules of play elicit. Respect, as Kant's *Critique of Practical Reason* and Ricoeur's *Fallible Man* have explicated, is what constitutes personal being as such. In an ideal game no one is forced to follow the rules, but everyone does so out of respect for those rules. Even in solitaire one recognizes that one is not really playing the game if one does not respect the rules.

It is in this way that Gadamer's hermeneutical theory puts us on the way to understanding what is meant by an underlying subject and how that subject is experienced. An additional step needs to be taken, however, inasmuch as the assertion "God is" has to do with the one *event* that underlies all events and not merely with an underlying subject. This has its parallel in the playing of games, but it involves a matter somewhat different from that of play as a subject. Not only can we play a game and be drawn into it; we can also *tell what happens* in a game. In telling what happens we are dealing with the game as an event rather than as a subject.

Thus, to tell what happened in a tennis game at Wimbledon in 1979 we might say, "Borg beat Tanner." This surface event, however, is pervaded by another event which takes place in and with it—an event that can be told in words which say in effect, "Tennis tennised." For these words designate what takes place, though not always manifested, whenever any particular tennis game is played. They tell what is always happening whenever any particular occurrence in tennis is taking place. Something more is said with the words "Tennis tennised" (or, more idiomatically but less exactly, "That was really tennis!") than is said by "Borg beat Tanner." That surplus of meaning is exactly the underlying event of tennis. When N played M, tennis tennised. "God is" similarly tells the event underlying all events whatsoever. It reaches still deeper than does an account of the tennising of tennis, in order to say what is happening in all events.

The subjectivity of a game is indicated by its power to draw us into its sphere and its power to command our respect for its form (the rules of playing). By contrast the event-character of a game is made known by its "donation" (its invitation to be appropriated), as indicated by its power to hold attention, to stay in the memory, and to awaken further expectation (or to put on the lookout for). To appear as an event a tennis match must show the capacity to hold attention, stay in the memory, and arouse further expectation. The excitement instilled by a close game can demonstrate both the subjectivity and the eventuality of the game. "That was a real match," which may express an intense respect, almost a reverence, for the game played, and "That was a memorable match," which expresses its being an event, can both record the excitement.

The same consideration applies to the event named with the words "God is." That the game, whose form is constituted by the rule that every action is to be ascribed to God and that in every action God is be-ing, is a subject is indicated by the power of this kind of movement of thought and word to draw us into it and to command respect for its form. But that there is also an event involved is indicated when the movement specified by the fundamental assertion "God is" shows a capacity to hold attention, stay in the memory, and awaken further expectation. "I want to see more" may, thus, give evidence of having experienced an event; it need not always be an expression of nosiness, that everyday form of curiosity which Heidegger analyzes in *Being and Time* as one of the marks of the fallenness of existence. The iteration "Let me see, let me see" that bespeaks idle curiosity is not the marvel "I want to see again and more" that registers a genuine response to an event.

In the assertion "God is," the movement which puts God's being into play is a movement of thought and language. (Whether a ritual can do the same is a matter that need not be treated here. There is no reason to preclude that possibility; but it does not affect the character of verification involved in testing whether it is true that "God is.") The assertion is a true narration of the event when the movement of language and thought itself makes manifest the character of event (by holding attention, staying in the memory, and arousing further expectation) and when the event so manifested accords with any and all other occurrences and events. These two conditions state the test of truth both as *aletheuein* and as correspondence.

We determine whether tennis is tennising in a particular game by watching or playing the game as specified by its rules. Similarly, to determine whether "God is," we watch or play the game of language and thought that is specified by the rules of theontic thinking—namely, that "God" is given the place of the subject of last resort, "is" is given the place of universal action, and "God is" designates what is always happening everywhere. Through watching or playing we see whether "Tennis is tennising" agrees with what we perceive to be happening; and, similarly, we see whether "God is" agrees with what we perceive to be happening in any event or occurrence whatever. If the event comes to light in the words, and if the time of the event agrees with the time manifested in other events, then "God is" is true; it is false if nothing comes to light and if the identity of time does not appear in the difference of occurrences.

This sense of "God is" has nothing directly to do with whether there exists something that is godly. In modern English it is not possible to interweave the two senses as is done in Aquinas's five ways (*S.th.*, 1,2,3). His *Deus est* is composed of an interplay between the existence of God and the be-ing of God as the one (the first) in the many (the secondary). The Latin *esse* held the *Deus datur* and the *Deus est* together so that Thomas could play now on the one and now on the other of the two senses without disrupting the intelligibility. Thus the *movens* of the first, "clearer" way means simultaneously the agent in any action and also the entity that acts upon another entity; and "prime mover" has the same double significance. *Movens* is the "mover" in any movement from potentiality to actuality as "walker" is in any walking, but it is also *aliquod ens*, some entity, that imparts motion to another entity.

Our senses ascertain, Aquinas begins, that things in this world move, or are changed from potentiality to actuality. So, for example, fire, which is hot in act, changes wood from being hot *in potentia* to being actually hot. But nothing can be both actual and potential in one and the same respect, and hence nothing can be both *movens* and moved. To be moved is to be moved by another. But since this sequence cannot proceed to infinity (otherwise there would be no first, and if no first, no second and no world at all), there must be a prime mover not moved by anything else. Everyone understands this as God. The very example that Thomas uses here makes the double sense of "mover" clear. Fire, which is actually hot, makes the wood hot. To be hot in act, that is, "to burn," is what fire always does; "fire" is to "burning" as "walker" is to "walking." When the fire makes the wood burn as well, then the relation between "the wood is burning" and "fire is burning" is like that between "Socrates is walking" and "a walker is walking" or between "a lamp is shining" and "light is shining." What "fires" the fire is not a cause of its burning in the same way as what "fires" the wood. What makes fire hot is still fire; what makes wood hot is something other than wood. The word "fire" already names a prime mover in "burning." Thus the "prime mover" that this way is to demonstrate is "prime," or "first," in the double sense of being the cause to which effects point back (as the heat of wood points to the burning of fire) and the subject of last resort for a certain action (as "fire" is what is always burning when anything burns, or light is what is always shining when anything shines).

The overt argument deals only with one of these two sides, and its validity depends in part upon shutting out the other side until the conclusion, which gives the meaning of God as the *primum movens.* The argument traces the hot wood to the fire; it may then trace the fire, not as heat in act, but as something else to what composes it. What the argument does not do is trace the relation of the intermediate agents to the one agent that is in all of them, e.g., "fire" as a prime mover of burning to "God" as a prime mover of be-ing. It does not trace that relation, but only, as it were, includes it in the naming of God that terminates each of the five ways of the demonstration: "Everyone understands God as the prime mover."

What unites these two senses in the language of Aquinas's five ways is the experience of the world which is at their basis. Through our sensation we experience the world as the connectedness of things with each other that is manifested in their movement; actualities point to potentialities. Together with this is an awareness of a fundamental division in being which separates things from each other. Nothing can be what it is both potentially and actually with respect to any one thing. Things are connected with each other by the significatory character of movement, but they are kept distinct from each other by the line between the potential and the actual. The very existence of things in connection, however, makes it both unnecessary and impossible for us (here the attention shifts from the world to the self) to trace the line of connection among things to infinity. The *procedere in infinitum* on our part is what the experience of the world precludes, and it precludes it as both unnecessary and impossible.

But this excluded possibility, designated in one way by reference to our mental action as a *procedere in infinitum*, is also designated by the titles "first mover," "first cause," etc., and by the name "God." That which is experienced and thought when one experiences the world in the connectedness of entities in movement, whose very appearance has always already excluded the infinite procedure, is the prime mover who is also called God. God appears in the world first as the negation of the need and the possibility of *procedere in infinitum*, then as an entity designated prime mover, and finally as the one named God. Ebeling calls this naming "a leap into the language of faith" ("Existenz," p. 100). That it is a movement within language, and not an inference, is clear; but it may be misleading to call the name that everyone uses the "language of faith." (It might be noted in passing that a serial proceeding to infinity is not ruled out, but only one which involves a gradation. It is not impossible to think that one human being depends on another human being, and so on, to infinity, but it is impossible to think the line from son to father to grandfather, and so on, without end [*S.th.*, 1,46,2 *ad* 7].)

3. "God Is G"

In the third reading, the assertion of the being of God is taken to be an incomplete predication. It has the sense "God is . . ." and requires that the missing predicate be filled in. But the predicate term is not a definer of the subject term, as it is in a normal judgments like "This is a tree" and "The leaf is green"; "God" is not a reference to a perceptible object but to a notion or word. In an objective judgment the predicate term provides a notion that defines the subject further, but it is the subject which makes primary reference to what is being spoken of. In "God is this one here," however, the structure is like that of "A tree is this" rather than that of "This is a tree." Such predications, in which the subject-term is the abstract notion and the predicate term the concrete percept, serve a different function. They do not answer the question "What is this?" Instead, they answer the question "Where is an example, or a concrete showing, of that to which reference is being made?" These predications, in other words, do not define, but they *point out*; they are ostensive rather than delimiting. "This is a tree" begins with the thing perceived and connects it to the abstract thought of the same; the ostensive predication "A tree is this," by contrast, begins with the abstract notion or the word and connects it with a perceptible object.

If "God is . . ." is understood as such an ostensive assertion, then its purpose is to point out where that which is thought of as God makes an appearance. It is to show how the notion of God appears to perception, or to point out what referent the name "God" can be applied to. If one has formed a concept of "tree" by reading a dictionary definition, one may ask for an object that exemplifies the notion. Similarly, the assertion "God is . . ." presupposes that we understand a certain notion contained in the word "God," but we are asking what person or thing or event will show how such a one appears concretely.

At first this distinction may seem to have no importance for verification; for if it is true that John is this man (one whom we point out), then it is also true that this man (the same one) is John. If it is true that a tree is this thing (which we point out), then it is also true that this same thing is a tree. Since "A tree is this" has the sense of "What we mean by the word 'tree' is exemplified by this object here," it follows that this object can be classified or at least named as a tree; hence, "This is a tree" is true if "A tree is this" is true.

But these relations are altered when what the ostensive saying involves is not an example but a symbol. If the "this" of "A tree is this" or "God is this" refers to an example of the kind of thing to which the term mentioned in the subject is applicable, then "A tree is this" and "This is a tree" are deducible from each other; if the one is true, the other is true as well. If, however, the thing that shows the referent is not an example but a *symbol of the essence* of that which the subject term names, then the two assertions are not implied by each other. Accordingly, if the term "tree" in "A tree is this" is understood not as a name or an abstract notion of a thing but rather as a concept of the *being* of what is so named, and thus as designating precisely that connection between singular (percept) and universal (notion) that is expressed by the word "is," then to say that a tree "is this" is to point out not an example of a quiddity but a symbol of an essence. Quiddity has to do with *what* something is; essence has to do with how, or *as what*, something is what it is. A symbol does not exemplify a quiddity; it makes an essence perceptible.

To see this distinction more clearly one may recall that an object-related thought (literal experience) is constituted by three elements: the percept, or the perceptible; the notion, or the cognizable; and the concept, or the conceptual, which makes a connection between the percept and the notion. Viewed from the side of the thinker, this third element is the act of conceiving (taking together); viewed with respect to the object, it is the object's reality. Both are designated by the word "being." In those ostensive assertions which have to do only with the percept and the notion (e.g., "What 'tree' [= the notion] means is this [= the percept]"), the defining assertion implies its converse ("This [= the percept] is a tree [= the notion]") because the notion states a property of the percept. In those which have to do with the concept of the object ("A tree is [what it is as] this"), such is not the case, because the percept is the essence, the manifest being, of the object. That is to say, if a perceived object does not exemplify the notion of that same object but manifests its being by showing what it means for that thing *to be* what it is, then it is symbolic instead of objective. In such a case it may be true that the perceived thing is a tree but false that a tree is to be classed as that kind of thing. If the notion of a tree is exemplified by a certain thing, then this thing bears the property of treehood— "tree" can be predicated of it. But if this thing manifests the being of a tree, then "tree" is neither a name the thing bears nor a property by which it is qualified but a capacity it has—the capacity to show what it means to be a tree, what it means that a tree is what it is and not something else. It makes perceptible that which we otherwise understand as the meaning of an assertion and ascertain as the reality of its reference.

The possibility of experiencing symbols depends upon the power of the referent of an assertion to do its own signifying of something else. When we understand the meaning of the assertion "This is a tree," we know what the assertion is about—the tree to which it refers. The signs of the sentence carry a meaning, and that meaning, or sense, signifies a referent. But, in turn, this referent may have a signifying power insofar as it leads us to ask what it means for that thing to be what it is. When a particular thing not only appears as the object to which an assertion refers ("This is a tree") but also shows what it means for a tree to be a tree (why it is just so and not otherwise), then the particular thing in question is a symbol as well as an objective referent. As an objective referent, it is that to which the assertion points because it is that *about* which the assertion is made. But as a symbol, it is also what being is all about. "What is this assertion *about?*" and "What is being a tree *all about?*" are two formulations indicating the first referent and the second referent—the referent signified by the linguistic signs and the referent signified by the first referent.

The double sense in language, to which Ricoeur refers and which at one point was central to his hermeneutics of symbols, has to do with the same structure. A symbol, Ricoeur wrote, is "any structure of signification in which a direct, primary, literal meaning designates, in addition, another meaning which is indirect, secondary, and figurative and which can be apprehended only through the first" ("Existence and Hermeneutics," p. 98). To this it should be added that the experience of truth depends upon there being in the literal reality a second reality as well that is apprehended through it. But which is the literal and which is the figurative does not matter as long as both meanings and both referents are recognized. It is possible to allow that in some situations what is figurative and what is literal are just the opposite of what they are in others. For the first sense of language lies in its power to signify objects that can be given to perception; the second sense lies in its power to let those signified objects in turn signify other realities (essences) given along with the perceptible objects.

This double signifying is the reason why the truth of "A tree is this" does not follow inferentially from "This is a tree," but depends upon whether the first or the second referent is intended through the assertion. It is possible, for example, that what shows the essence of a tree (and what is, therefore, the basis for saying "A tree is this") is not a tree at all but, say, a log at a fireplace or the fire burning in the fireplace. The intention of the assertion may be to say that the burning of the fire and giving of

warmth express what it means for a tree to be a tree—it means to
be capable of lighting a hearth or warming a room. Obviously
the assertion "This is a tree" would be false in these circumstances, while "A tree is this" would be true. The log is a symbol
of the being of the tree, though it is not a tree. As such a symbol
it is a second referent in the literal referent, so that the statement
"This is a tree" signifies an object, but this object signifies a second referent, a power or capacity (to warm a hearth and light a
room) which is embodied in the log at the fireplace.

The distinction between an object and a symbol (a log that is
just that, and a log that is the essence of a tree) is made by
reflection. Prereflective relations involve symbols but not the experience of symbols as such, that is, as different from literal
objects. Without the capacity for reflection—the self's relating
itself to its relation–to—a distinction between the entity as the
referent of an assertion and the entity as the bearer of an essence
cannot be made. An assertion points to an object as its referent,
which is the "about-what" of the assertion. That object in turn, as
a synthesis of perceptual and cognizable elements, points to
being as it appears in this particular place; and as thus pointing
to an essence, the object is not only a referent of the assertion but
also a signifier of another referent, which is the essence embodied there. The essence, as the second referent, can be paraphrased as a capacity (the capacity of warming a hearth and
lighting a room) that is the meaning of a thing's being what it is
("what it means for a tree to be a tree is to . . ."). A sentence has a
meaning (carried by the linguistic signs), but an entity also has a
meaning (carried by its appearance as a signifier of essence).

The verification of an assertion about a symbol is correspondingly different from that of an assertion about an object.
Whether an assertion about a symbol ("A tree is this") is true
depends upon whether the thing ("this") does actually show the
essence that is named in the subject-term of the assertion. The
sense of the assertion is that a tree is what it is *as* this-thing-here
and that this-thing-here accordingly shows what it means for a
tree to be what it is at all. A thing that is a symbol shows essence

rather than quiddity. If it shows the essence, then it says, not, "This is what is meant by the word or idea 'tree,' " but, "There one can see what it means for a tree to be a tree at all." It serves as a sign carrying a meaning which points to the being that is the essence of a thing. To see that the *meaning of an assertion* is the same as the reality of an object is to experience truth upon that object; to see that the *meaning of an object* is the same as the reality of the object (though meaning is distinct from reality) is to experience truth upon a symbol.

We determine whether a thing has certain properties ("this is a tree," "the leaf is green") by what we can see—with our eyes, our intuitive perception of form, or through some measuring instrument. We determine whether a thing shows the essence, or being, of what it names by what we can understand in view of the object. If, for example, the response to a particular thing is to think or say, "It makes sense for a tree to have branches if to be a tree means to be able to offer protection and refuge," then in view of this object we can understand the being of a tree. The essence (in this case, the capacity of offering protection and refuge) is what is shown by the particular object; that capacity is the second referent, which is contained in the first referent, the perceived object tree, and which we become aware of as an understanding. This is what seeing that the meaning of the object is the same as the reality of the object amounts to.

These considerations can now be applied to the verification of the assertion "God is *G*" (where *G* designates a perceptible entity). When the sense of the assertion is not that *G* exemplifies what is meant by the notion of God but that *G* is a place at which the essence of God—how, or as what, God is who and what he is—is shown, then the assertion does not necessarily imply that *G* has divine properties. Thus, the christological statement that God is Jesus of Nazareth (illustrated, for example, by the Pauline words that God was "in Christ reconciling" the world) does not imply that Jesus of Nazareth has divine properties or deity as a predicate. It asserts, rather, that it is the man Jesus who shows what it means for God to be God; and even if this demonstration of God is final and full—so that to see God there is to see in an unsurpassable way how the deity is the deity it is—still the man Jesus is the place at which the deity appears in its deity, but deity is not necessarily a predicate applicable to him. The deity is the deity it is *as* this man. Whether "God is Jesus" is true is determined not by whether Jesus has divine properties but by whether Jesus the man is the essence of God, that is to say, by whether in view of the man Jesus we can understand what it means for God to be God. For Jesus to be the symbol of the essence of God means for his career to signify and make manifest what it means for God to be God. One can understand why Jesus' career ran the course it did if the essence of God, what it means for God to be God, is to be other than God.

"God Is God"

A special problem for verification is posed by the tautology "God is God." In this, as in other tautologies, what is asserted may be nothing (when the tautology is "empty") or the identity of being (when the tautology is "significant").[2] But the peculiar difficulty of "God is God" lies elsewhere, in the question whether a distinction can be made between what is asserted significantly by this tautology as compared with any other tautology and, further, whether a distinction can be made between what this assertion refers to and the whole thinking-being process. In the speculative idealist interpretation "God is God" is equivalent to "God is the absolute process." In the interpretation on the part of negative theology, of which Josef Hochstaffl's *Negative Theologie* (pp. 188-223) is a contemporary representative although not explicitly related to the issues being treated here, "God is God" is equivalent to "God is the negation of everything and of nothing." The problem posed by the former interpretation can be treated first.

The nature of this problem can be delineated by reference to the role played by thinking and being in the Western metaphysical tradition. The word "thinking" has been used to designate the basic activity through which we consciously relate ourselves to an other. Dreamily gazing at objects without being conscious of them as such is not a matter of thinking; but willing and planning something, conversing, working out problems, intuiting things, seeing rational forms, and composing poems are. In this same tradition the word "being" is used to designate the correlate of thinking; it includes things perceived as well as things thought and conceived. What thinking is fundamentally concerned with is always being. Why this is so need not be discussed here; the point is only that underlying the experience of objects is always a *thinking of being*.

This relation becomes complicated in the case of human entities, where an act of thinking is at the same time a matter of being. What characterizes the being of human beings (*Dasein* or *anima aeterna*) is that being and thinking are the same. With respect to other entities our thinking is different from their being what they are. But with respect to ourselves our thinking is the same as our being what we are; in our thinking we are being ourselves. Being always involves a connection between singularity and universality. The being of an object is that factor in it which enables us to conceive of it by connecting a percept with a notion. Our own being as a self is our own thinking; for it is our thinking that makes the connection betwen the universality and the singularity by which we are constituted as human selves. How we think of ourselves and other things is the same as how we are who we are because, for *anima aeterna* or *Dasein,* the universal to which each is related on its singular own (" 'I' am this-one-here") is not a natural species but the possibility of relating the self in thought to any entity at all and to all entities together. Of distinctively human beings, therefore, one can say that *thinking is being*—the activity of relating ourselves (thinking) to an other and to a whole—is at the same time that to which we relate ourselves (being) and also that to which others, in thinking of us, relate themselves (being).

A further step can be taken. If in the first place we distinguish between thinking and being and in the second place identify the two in human being, then in the third place we can also inquire about the being of thinking. What *is* thinking? As indicated, it is more than an activity each self performs as its own; it is a universal process in which each participates. It "is" a process in which a subject consciously relates itself to an other. Thus, to the extent that we are aware of thinking we are aware not only of our own being but also of a universal process that is independent of our particular being. There is a being to thinking that is other than our own individual being. What that being is can be articulated by the logical principles in their systematic connection. A book on systematic logic, accordingly, provides an abstract picture of the *being of thinking*.

Finally—to take the last step—reflexive thought is a process in which *being is thinking*, that is to say, a process in which thinking is both the activity and also the object of that activity. "Being" designates what is other than thinking and is the normal concern or subject matter of thinking. But in reflexive thought that concern is thinking itself. Hence, the conception of *reflexivity*, like that of *Dasein* (or human being), provides an identification of being and thinking. In reflexivity, however, the identification is absolute— one is thinking only about the thinking process itself. But this absoluteness, in which being (what one is thinking of) is thinking, is also what is meant by the *being of God*. As Daub put it, when one reflects on the notion of God, one sees that the essence of God is being as thinking and the existence of God is thinking as being (*Vorl.*, VI, p. 63). Thus, in reflexive thinking, where being is thinking and thinking is being, we have arrived at what is the being of God. "God is God" comes, in the end, to say the same as "being is thinking," which defines reflexivity; and reflexive thinking is a participation in God's being God, a manifestation that God is God.

This line of thought—from the thinking of being to thinking as being and from the being of thinking to being as thinking—is nothing else than a restatement of the Hegelian conception of the relation between humanity and God. In the end, absolute thinking (here called reflexivity) is the being of God himself. For that reason a *Science of Logic*, as Hegel developed it, is also a theological treatise; "one can say that this content [logic as the system of pure reason] is the portrayal [*Darstellung*] of God as he is in his eternal essence before the creation of nature and finite spirit" (*WdL*, I, p. 44). And a phenomenology of mind is the same as the revelation of the being of God. In the end we have the same reality that we had at the beginning; namely, that God is God. Between-times the task is to see that what we are aware of as our own thinking is a finite expression of the absolute that is God's being God. Whether called "speculative thinking" or "God's being," it is the same process. For a human being to think reflexively and for God to be God are one and the same act. The only difference is that some people are able to see this identity, others are able to believe it though not to see it, and still others are able neither to believe nor to see it. The purpose of the elevation of consciousness is to make it possible to see that our thinking of things—our relating of ourselves to our world—is the creativity, in finite form, of God's being God; the being of God is the infinite process of which the particular acts are finite expressions.

For all of its appeal—and one should not deny that it does have a great attractiveness—this panentheism, by not distinguishing the whole thinking of being from the being of God, does not reckon with the possibility that God is other than even the absolute process. Is the identity in being and thinking the absolute dimension of thinking itself, and nothing more, or is it also the sign of a reality other than thought? This is, basically, the question with which Schelling after 1827 undertook to dethrone the Hegelian absolute. Being-itself (or the absolute structure constituted by thinking and being together) is not God, he declared, but only the material for God's being. God is the one who can both be and not be God. He is the freedom that is prior to being and thinking. In a similar fashion dialectical theology in the 1920s spoke of the "wholly other" God, the God who, in the train of Schelling's thought and Kierkegaard's language, is known as "wholly other" than the absolute.

One can now see how these attacks upon absolute idealism

amount to an interpretation in which "God is the reflexive process itself" has the sense that reflexive thinking shows what it means for God to be God. Reflexivity (Schelling: being-itself) is the symbol of the being of God, but it is not itself the being of God. Relating oneself to one's relations (reflexivity) is what it means for God to be God. Thus the verification of "God is God" depends upon whether reflexivity does show what it means for God to be God. The connection between a particular thought of a particular thing and the whole thinking-being process is the connection between finite and infinite; but the connection between that process itself and the being of God is the connection between a symbol and the referent of the symbol. The referent of the symbol is the essence, the what-it-means-to-be, in the symbol itself. If the thinking-being process is a symbol of the being of God, then it shows what it means for God to be God. But it is, as such, other than God. What it *means* to be God (the one in the many) is to be able to relate oneself to one's other. But to *be* God is to be other than the process of relating oneself to one's other, which is the being of thinking.

The terms that are synonymous in this account are "being-itself," "absolute being," "the absolute," "the absolute process," "the being of thinking," and "the reflexive process." The question at issue is whether "God is God" says anything more than that the absolute is the absolute, etc. If not, the being of God is no different from the being of thinking, or the absolute process of reflexivity. But if "God is God" has the sense that God is God *as* the absolute process, then the being of thinking shows what it means for God to be God even though reflexivity is not itself the divine being. The being of thinking and the being of God are different, but the being of thinking is capable of showing what it means for God to be God.

The verification of "God is God" (i.e., the absolute process) in this symbolic sense depends upon whether the absolute process does show what it means for God to be God. That the self *is the self by relation to another* (i.e., by thinking of being) makes sense if what it means for God to be God is to be himself by relating himself to his other; that the thinking of thinking is the thinking of the being of thinking (reflexivity) makes sense if what it means for God to be God is to be himself by relating himself to his other. These are ways of formulating the criterion that is applied in the verification, and they are an indication that the doctrine of the Trinity in Christian theology is an expression of the God signified by the process of thinking of being. To say that the activity makes sense is to say that it carries a meaning which signifies a referent, a referent which, in this case, is God. If it does "make sense" to think reflexively, then that "God is God" is true is confirmed. Whether it does make sense to do so is determined in the same way that one determines whether an assertion makes sense—it makes sense if we can apprehend a meaning ("understand") in the perceptible signs. In sentences and assertions, the signs are the acoustic or visual figures of a language; in activities—as in the reflexive process—the sign is the figure of the activity itself as that figure is given in the language (in a grammatical or logical form) or as it might be given in a mental representation that we make of the activity. The activity of judgment, for example, is figured in the patterns S-P and pS as well as in the picture of dividing and putting together (*ur-teilen*, *Urteil*; *divisio*, *conclusio*). Whether an activity not only signifies a further referent but also presents that referent is a separate question to which attention will be given in the next chapter. For the moment it is sufficient to observe that "God is God" is true to the extent that reflexivity is a significant activity, for what it then signifies is the being of God as the referent contained in the activity itself.

The verification of statements about reflexivity is one matter. They can be seen to be true to the extent that what is said about the activity corresponds with what the activity is. The verification of statements about God as the absolute is another matter. They are seen to be true to the extent that the activity of reflexive thought "makes sense" or is a significant activity; for in that event it shows the essence of God, or what it means for God to be God. For thinking to be what it is, and for God to be God, are the same at the point where the meaning of thinking and the meaning of the being of God come together.

The difference in wording needs to be noted carefully. What it means for thinking to be thinking is a question like what it means for a tree to be what it is. The intention of the question is to discover a sense, or meaning, in the reality of the object under attention. In the case of a tree that meaning may be provided by a log at a fireplace (in the example used earlier), which says that what it means for a tree to be a tree is to be able to provide light and warmth. In the case of thinking, the meaning is provided by whatever images or other reactions are evoked by the word "God." This is to say that what it means for thinking to be what it is, is for it to be able to name itself in another way.

There is a second sense to the assertion "God is God" that requires attention, for it makes possible a distinction between "God is God" and "Being is being." Thus far the assertion has been interpreted as saying that the reflexive process shows the being of God. But the test which determines that "God is God" is true will simultaneously determine that "Being is being" is true, since it is the showing of being in pure identity that provides the meaning for the activity of reflexive thinking. Thinking is other than being, as well as it is other than God; and if reflexivity is seen to make sense because God's being means that he relates himself to what is other than God, this will simultaneously hold for being—reflexivity makes sense if what it means for being to be itself is to be related to what is other than being, namely, to thinking. In the second interpretation, the sense of "God is God" is related to the power of negating, of saying "no" to, and of saying "not" about, things. Here the contrast between thinking as the affirmation of being (thinking things as they are) and thinking as the negation of being (thinking of them as they are not) makes possible the distinction between "Being is being" and "God is God" as the second referent of which reflexivity is the symbol. That God is *God* means he is *not* this-thing-here or any other thing or person or idea; the being of God is shown by our power to negate anything and everything. Augustine's interrogation of creation is based on this recognition (*Conf.*, 10:6,9). Asked who God is, each created thing replies, as do all things together, "We are not he, but he made us." When "God is God" is said so as to imply that God is *not* I, *not* this, that, or anything else, then what shows the godliness of God is the power of negation. "God is God" has the sense, "God is God *as* the power of negation that is actualized in anyone's No's and Not's." "God is God" is parallel to "Being is being," but it enunciates the second referent in our activity of negating, whereas "Being is being" enunciates the second referent in our activity of affirming. That I can say "not" and "no" makes sense if God is God; that I can say "yes" and make a positive judgment makes sense if Being is being.

If what it means for God to be God is to be other than anything and everything, then our making judgments not only affirmatively ("This is a tree") but also negatively ("This is not a bush, etc., ad infinitum") points to the being of God as that which it signifies. The truth of the assertion, which is tautological in form, lies in the correspondence between what we can understand in view of the negating activity and what is shown by that activity. In "God is Jesus" it is the man Jesus who shows what it means for God to be God; namely, to be other than God. In "God is God, i.e., not anything else," it is the "not" that shows what it means for God to be God—it means to be other than any subject or object. "To show the essence of God" and "to make sense if God is . . ." correspond to each other. If it is true that thinking or saying "not" and "no" shows what the essence of God is, then the truth lies in the correspondence between what it shows and what it makes possible to understand.

Just as we can understand the sense carried by the linguistic signs of an assertion, so we can understand the sense carried by a reality or by our activity as a sign. The activity of negating has sign-character to the extent that it provokes the question "What does it mean that we can in principle say No and Not to anything and everything?" Our activity of negation shows the being of God to the extent that this activity makes sense if God is *God* and no thing or person.

In summary, "God is this" is true when what "this" refers to does symbolize the meaning of God's being God. That it does symbolize the meaning is determined by whether, in view of the symbol, we can understand why it is as it is and not otherwise. Thus, "God is Jesus" is true when Jesus does symbolize the meaning of God's being God—the essence of God. That Jesus does so symbolize the essence of God is determined by whether (a) the career or figure of Jesus prompts us to ask "What does it mean?" and (b) when, in view of this same career or figure, we can say, "This makes sense if for God to be God is to be other than God." (As Rahner put it, man is what God becomes when he shows himself in the region of the extra-divine ["Anonymous," p. 393]. To this one must add, and to show himself in the region of the extra-divine is what it means for God to be God.)

Similarly "God is the absolute process (reflexivity)," or "God is God" (in the first sense), is true if reflexivity shows what it means for God to be God. This is determined by (a) whether the absolute process of reflexivity prompts us to ask, "What does it mean that we can think about thinking and thus seek being in thinking?" and (b) whether, in view of reflexive thought (that is, as we are aware of it when engaged in it or recalling it afterward), we can say, "This makes sense if for God to be God is to relate himself to what is other than himself, or, in short, to be trinitarian."

Finally, "God is *God*, i.e., not-I and not-this" is true (a) when our ability to say "not" and "no" about and to anyone and anything prompts us to ask, "What does it mean that we can negate unlimitedly?" and (b) when, in view of our actual negating (that is, as we are aware of it while engaging in it or recalling it afterward), we can say, "This makes sense if for God to be God is to be just different."

When it is the meaning of *words* that points to a referent, truth is experienced as the correspondence between the sense of the words and the reality of the object. When it is the meaning of the *object* (the first referent) that points to a second referent, truth is the correspondence between the meaning of the reality and the showing of the potentiality (possibility) in that object. "This is a tree" is experienced as true when what we understand the words to say corresponds to how the reality to which that meaning refers appears, or shows itself. "A tree is this" (where "this" designates a symbol instead of an example of treehood) is experienced as true when what we understand the reality of this thing to signify ("What does it mean?") corresponds to how the possibility, or potentiality, to which it points conditions the reality (as that which makes it have sense—"This makes sense if to be means . . ."). By distinguishing these two kinds of assertions one can see how a log at a fireplace might embody the essence of a tree ("What it means for a tree to be a tree is to be capable of giving warmth and light") even though it is not an example of a tree. In this case the second referent (the essence of tree) given with the first referent (the log) is capable of being given as a first referent as well—as a tree about which one speaks as directly as one speaks about a log. But in other cases, such as in the assertion "God is this," the second referent ("God") is given only with the direct referent ("this"), as that which conditions, and endows with sense, the reality (as in the figure of Jesus) or the activity (as in reflexive thinking or in negating) of the first reference.[3]

3

"God Is": *Truth and the Schism of Reflection*

All appearance indicates neither a total exclusion nor a manifest presence of divinity, but the presence of a God who hides himself. Everything bears this character.
— Pascal, *Pensées*, p. 9

He was buried, and rose again; the fact is certain because it is impossible.
— Tertullian, *De carne Christi*, c.5

He is his word going forth from silence.
— Ignatius, *Mag.*, 8:2

When the patterns of verification set forth in the preceding chapter are applied to the assertion that God is, the results are diverse. From the standpoint of reflection, the assertion that there is someone or something that possesses divine attributes ("God is" in the sense of "God exists" or "There is one that is God") can only be experienced as false; "God is" as the manifestation of the event underlying all events is experienced unclearly today; and "God is this-one-here" is experienced clearly as both true and false.

Deity and Existence
"There is something or someone that is God" is experienced as untrue because no object of possible experience can be judged to have the properties of deity. Reflection and the experience of the existence of God are in this way incompatible with each other.

94

For it lies in the nature of God to be the judge and not the judged; and it lies in the nature of reflection that "I," or not God, occupy the position of judge. The standpoint of reflection is that from which I compare what can be seen in the relation between the meaning that is understood in signs and the reality that is given as corresponding or not corresponding to that meaning. If there is to be an experience of the truth of the assertion that there exists something that is God, then the reflecting subject must be able to see that the one referred to as God possesses the properties signified by the name or designation "God." In reflection the final judging subject is the reflecting "I," and not that about which the judgment is being made. The very structure of this experience excludes, therefore, the possibility that anything could be seen to be God. To put it precisely: one could experience the assertion of the existence of God as true only by seeing that the one intended by the name "God" cannot be judged by the reflecting subject, but if reflection cannot judge what it sees then it cannot experience what truth might be there. Consequently, the assertion that something exists as God can never be true for a reflecting subject. To say that it is true is to say something that defeats the sense of the word "true"; for that an assertion is true means that its meaning can be seen to correspond with what is so.

This recognition lay behind the polemic against religion on the part of dialectical theology in the 1920s. (See Jenson, *God*, pp. 39-40; 80; 124.) Barth understood religion to be the quest for God based on the presupposition that the one who seeks God can tell both that he has not yet found God and that he can judge when he finds God. Religion rests on the presumption that it is possible for the religious person to recognize that something is God if that divine something should ever be found. Used in this sense, "religion" designates the belief, with its accompanying attitude and practice, that there is something or someone that discernibly (if only to the "eyes of faith") possesses the properties of deity and that can therefore be called, and worshiped as, God. But this—so the theological polemic—represents the ultimate denial of God, for under the title of "religion" it preserves the judging position of the "I" engaged in the religious quest or practice. Religion and the belief that something is divine go together. If religion were true, then one should be able to see that what is asserted to be divine does indeed have divine properties. But reflection sees just the opposite—that everything presented as divine is not so because it can be subjected to a reflective judgment. A religion that proceeds on the assumption that we could readily tell who God is if only he were to appear, or on the assumption that the "eyes of belief" can see truth where reflection cannot, is in the end nothing more than a deluded reflection. The reflective experience connected with the assertion that something is God is always "atheistic." The notion of God is an infinite idea to which nothing can ever correspond. Consequently, what can be experienced as true is that nothing is God rather than that something is, or may be, God. "This one is God" can only be experienced as false or untrue.

A part of this same recognition may lie behind Tillich's position that, strictly speaking, God does not "exist": "If 'existence' refers to something which can be found in the whole of reality, no divine being exists" (*DF*, p. 47). For the denial of existence to deity is not only due to the special meaning which the word "existence" acquired through existentialism; it also rests on the conflict between reflection and religion, which is at the heart of Tillich's early philosophy of religion and systematic theology. Most succinctly that conflict is set forth in his article "Philosophie und Religion" published in the 1930 edition of *Religion in Geschichte und Gegenwart*, where it is formulated as the conflict between religion as a "pure being-grasped" and philosophy as "radical questioning." Both of the two opponents can transcend themselves when the "radical being-grasped" that is their common basis is made apparent, but even in this self-transcendence the proposition that something exists that has properties of deity cannot be seen to be true. The contradiction between religion and reflection seems to be pure. "The religious person believes he can escape philosophy [radical questioning] since, as a possessor of truth, he does not need to ask; and the philosopher believes he must keep religion at a distance, since it would hinder radical questioning by its pregiven truth" (*GW*, V, p. 101).

Tillich sees a solution to this apparently pure conflict in the circumstance that religion incorporates a critical moment, insofar as it recognizes that the concrete form in which the unconditioned appears is inadequate to what that form expresses; this is the element of radical questioning in religion. Similarly, there is an element of unquestionability, or of the unjudged, in the radical questioning of reflection, insofar as any critique is directed toward something concrete, something given; it is a questioning of something that is in advance there. The assertion that there is a God, for example, is always made by someone, whose word is questionable. That is the concrete and questionable element in religion. On the other hand, that one can question whether *God* is, or whether there is an unquestionable, indicates that the religious referent is given at least in the form of that which is questioned. That reflection depends upon an initially unreflected datum and that religion has to do with a questionable form of the unconditioned are indications of where the two converge—in "the unity of the unconditioned and the concrete" (or, in theological terms, the unity of the divine and human). In the nature of the case, however, this unity can never be given as such to reflection.

The incompatibility between deity and a judgment of existence is a theme common to the early Barth and Tillich. The difference is that Barth specifies it as the negation of religion by the revealed God, and Tillich, as the negation of the God of theology by the principle of unconditionedness in actual religion. For Barth God is the negation of the God of the religious question; for Tillich the religious principle embedded in concrete religions is the negation of the theological concept of God. In either case it is impossible to ascertain that an existent is God.

The negative result applies as well to the statement "Jesus is God" or to any similar statement. Such an assertion can never be experienced as true because reflection can never ascertain whether the subject named does have the properties of divinity. The problem does not derive from the particular content of the statements; it is rooted in reflection itself. In this matter, indeed, reflection and prophetic criticism, or what Tillich called the prophetic, or Protestant, principle, concur. This principle states that the claim of anything which purports to be or appears to be God is to be denied. No entity and no appearance can be God, for God transcends the world and the self radically. As expressed in the biblical tradition, this principle seems to exempt from its stricture the phenomenon of the word—a command can be heard as a divine command even though no entity or person can be judged to be divine; Abraham and the prophets can hear a word from the Lord. But even this apparent exception is drawn into the negation when hearing becomes as self-critical as does seeing. If, upon hearing the summons of God to leave his native land and later to sacrifice his son Isaac, Abraham had asked whether the command he heard was indeed the command of God, he would have had to reply in the negative; for the very ability to put the question is a symptom that no affirmative answer can be based in experience. Something can appear as God, and a word can be heard as the word of God and in that way experienced as God, only until the question is raised whether the apparition and the audition are in truth of God. (The problem involved in ascertaining whether a command is a divine command is not different from that of determining whether something is God.)

Kerygmatic theology, under either a Barthian or Bultmannian inspiration, only apparently eludes this stricture. Thus, Heinrich Vogel states that a theological assertion is true when it meets these criteria: Its referent is Jesus as the Logos of God, for he is the one who as a man "speaks this 'I am [the truth]' as *only God* can speak it"; it is an answer to the word of God that has been heard, for it is true "only by virtue of *God's self-assertion*, [and] as an *answer* to the word of God spoken to us through the mouth of the one who hears it [sc., a prophet or apostle who, unlike the rest of us, hears it immediately]"; and it is true "in that instant which is determined by the *presence* of the one who himself is the truth" ("Wahr," pp. 180, 186, and 187, emphasis in text).

What this amounts to can be seen in three examples that Vogel adduces. The statement "God justifies sinners" is not true as a general statement about what God does; it is true only "when God discloses himself . . . as the God who here and now is justifying the godless one" (p. 188). Transferred to the assertion "God is," this account would say that "God is" is not true as a general statement about what is always going on, but it is true at those times when the event of the being of God is made manifest. Vogel's observation thus coincides with the description that "God is" can be formally correct without actually revealing the unity of events which it formulates. Its real truth can be seen only when "God discloses himself," that is, when the event that is formulated by the words is made manifest.

Similarly, in a second example, John's declaration "God is love" (1 John 4:16) is not true as a general description of the nature of God. It is true, Vogel says, only when we hear it as John's answer to the self-manifestation of God; that is to say, when in and through John's words "God is love" what we actually hear is an "I love" on the part of God. Finally, the assertion "God is God" is not to be understood as a tautology but as the statement that "*that* God who gives, imparts, and communicates himself in Jesus Christ through the Holy Spirit is God"; "God is God in that he is the Father, . . . the Son, . . . the Spirit" (p. 187).

It was a contribution of great value when kerygmatic theology, which Vogel's essay represents, saw that language can not only signify a meaning but also present a reality (in an announcing person rather than, as in empirical science, in an appearing object or, as in ethics, in the other person's demand for respect of his freedom), or more particularly, that it can present the power to be what one could not be without that annunciation. It can present as reality an existence which appears otherwise only as a possibility. This recognition was behind Bultmann's contention that existentialist analytics, as carried out in Heidegger's *Being and Time*, could describe inauthenticity and authenticity as modes of being but could not enable a self actually to become authentic. In different terms this also lay behind Heidegger's recognition at the end of the analytics that something else is needed; from the meaning of existence as temporality one cannot uncover the meaning of being, but from a disclosure of being one might illuminate the meaning of existence. The leap from the meaning of being-there to the meaning of being could not be made unless being first disclosed itself in the announcements of poetry.

"Kerygma," in its technical sense, is the kind of announcing which presents the reality of which it speaks. Accordingly, the role of "God is love"—to use Vogel's example—or of "Jesus was raised" (in Bultmann's theology) is not that of an assertion which carries a meaning that projects a referent to be ascertained; it is, instead, that of a declaring which presents the referent signified by some other assertion. It provides the donation of reality that corresponds to a projection of reality made through other assertions; the realities that are otherwise only existential possibilities appear as real in the announcing person. The general statement "God is love" must be distinguished from the Kerygma "God is love." The former carries a sense which signifies a referent; the latter gives a referent, a reality for a sense. The kerygmatic assertion "God is love" is true if, in a person who is announcing "God is love" to us, the love of God is really presented. "God is love" is true because the announcement to us by another is actually heard as the reality of love on the part of the one who, though not the same as the announcing person, is speaking at the same time.

Similarly, in Bultmann's conception of Jesus as resurrected "into the kerygma," the role of the announcement "Jesus was raised from the dead" is not that of an assertion which projects, but that of the donation which presents, the referent. It presents the reality, by its actually enabling the hearer to be a self authentically, and this reality corresponds to what is projected through an assertion about human possibility. Such a mediation of real power in the kerygma is not the same as a psychological effect.

That a hearer of the kerygma of the resurrection is enabled to accept the situation of existence as his very own doing (and thereby to be who he is authentically) is not a psychological trans-formation, but the actual reception of a donation of power from without the hearing person. Of course, psychological changes may accompany such a reception; but that is not what defines the nature of the kerygma, and its reality does not depend upon such changes. The reality that is presented through the an-nouncing person, the *keryx*, is as much external to the recipient as is the reality of an appearing object. Both are data, or donations, to experience.

What obscures this similarity is the circumstance that the mediating role of language with respect to appearances of ob-jects has been forgotten. A physical object is not given apart from language altogether, say, through a silent gazing upon a loca-tion; it is shaped as an object by the way in which it is put into words. The green leaf as we see it with our eyes is the object "in itself," in contrast to what it is in an assertion about it. But we see the object in itself, instead of being dreamily presented with a stretch of sensation, only because it has been put into words. It is already called a leaf before any of us perceives it. In this sense Wittgenstein's observation about material objects is correct. We do not define the concept of a material object as "what is really seen" rather than what appears in language; instead, "what we have rather to do is to 'accept' the everyday language-game, and to note 'false' accounts of the matter 'as' false" (Holmer, *Gram-mar*, p. 206). "The primitive language game which children are taught," Wittgenstein continues, "needs no justification; at-tempts at justification need to be rejected." All of this is to say that primitive objectivity is not a matter of the silent presence of things but of a presence mediated through the language which treats them as such.

From this point of view the opposition between the kerygmatic and the scientific account of truth is less sharp than it might otherwise appear; for a parallel can be sketched between the role of language with respect to the reality projected by "The leaf is green" and that presented by "Jesus is resurrected." On the one hand, we can understand the sense of "The leaf is green" and "Jesus is no longer dead (is resurrected)" just by hearing the sentences spoken or by reading them. We can understand each of them without knowing whether they are true. To determine that they are true is to ascertain that the leaf to which reference is made *is* green and that Jesus *is* indeed living. But the place where we find the deed in which the leaf is what it is and Jesus is what he is is not free of language. What happens is that in view of the leaf referred to we can say, "The leaf is indeed green." In view of the leaf we are presented with an object through our physical senses mediated by the same words as those used to make the intelligible assertion about it.

The parallel to this presentation in kerygmatic language is the confrontation with the words through the voice of some other human speaker. The green leaf is presented as an object when the language used to interpret what we are seeing is the same as the language that was understood when the assertion was made about it. But we are presented with the living Jesus when the language used to interpret what a hearer is actually enabled to be as he attends to the words said to him agrees with the language initially understood in the assertion. In other words, "I can be the self that I am" is true because it corresponds to what happens when I hear announced to me "Jesus is resurrected." Listening to the kerygma of the resurrection is a way of ascertaining whether what has been said about human possibility is so. This act of listening to what is announced by another person is, in the kerygmatic framework, what the act of beholding an object through our sensation is.

The parallel is obscured because looking at the tree seems to be wordless, whereas listening to the kerygma is not so. But this is not the case. One must distinguish between the words which present the real power to be and the words in which assertions are made about that power. "Jesus is resurrected" is a language in which the power to be one's own self on one's own makes its appearance; it is on a par with the physical shape, color, size, and so on of the leaf that presents itself through sensation. The conception of pure beholding without the mediation of language may apply to dreamlike images but not to the perception of physical objects. The two become confused because it is possible to remember the dreamlike state after it has passed. Accordingly, as kerygma "Jesus is resurrected" is not the assertion whose truth is to be tested against reality. For the words represent the in-itself of the real power to which the existential assertion "I can be the self that I am on my own" makes reference. The assertion to be verified is this one: "I can be the self that I am." It is true if, when I hear announced to me "Jesus was raised from the dead," I can appropriate the power and actually be the self I am. The statement about Jesus *gives* what the statement about the self *projects*.

Drawing the parallel in this way does, admittedly, neglect the question of how the "self" that I am can be the same as the "Jesus" of the kerygma "Jesus is resurrected." That question, however, has to do with a theory about the relation between being a self and being Jesus, between what is expressed as "I" and what is expressed as "the Christ." Such a theory may explain, but it would not change, the actual experience of the identity between the self that "I" can be and the one that is named as Jesus the Christ in the kerygma. This identity is expressed in the "I am" attributed to Jesus in the New Testament; every saying of "I am" is a participation in his being.

The leaf as it appears through the language which reads it is the leaf in itself; and this stands in contrast to the leaf as it appears in the assertion about the leaf which can be understood apart from its actual appearing to the senses. When what that understanding projects and what the appearance presents can be put into the same words, the assertion is true. The projection may take the form of an image, so that when one hears the words "The leaf is green" one forms a picture of a green leaf which is then compared with how the object to which it refers presents itself through sensation. But understanding meanings includes more than the formation of such mental pictures, as William

James's example of Memorial Hall made clear.

Similarly, the power to be the self I am on my own, as it is presented through the announcing person, is that power in itself, in contrast to the power as anticipated in the assertion of possibility "I can be the self I am on my own." The phrase "in itself" refers to a state independent of my action upon the thing or the power. The means by which we have access to that state varies with the nature of the reality. With mundane objects it is through sensation; with powers of subjectivity it is through hearing another speak. For a leaf to *be* green in reality means for it to present itself to physical sensation in a certain way. To "be" the self that I am means to appropriate one's self on one's own. It means to be able to say of the self presented in the words of the kerygma "That is I," or "I am that one." The kerygma of Jesus as Christ does not say, "You cannot be yourself authentically, therefore Christ must be it for you," but it presents, outside me, the self that "I" really am as a power to be appropriated. It thereby confirms, or verifies, the assertion "I can be the one I am on my very own" by making the possibility actual.

Without having explicated it in this manner, kerygmatic theology did make appeal to the capacity of language to present a referent as well as to project it or interpret it; and this insight is encapsulated in the notion of kerygma. Even this, however, will not provide reflection with a means for determining that what is heard through the other person's announcement that "God is love" is the speaking of God and that the words of the other person are the word of God. Vogel may assert that Jesus speaks the words "I am the truth" as only God can, but no criterion is provided—indeed none can be provided—by which to determine whether someone speaks "as only God can." For the question of whether there is an identity between the herald and God is not subject to verification by reflection as is the identity between the selfhood of anyone who is "I" and the self presented in the kerygma about Jesus. This latter is experientially verifiable without forsaking the standpoint of reflection because it is possible to see that the possibility projected as authentic existence is the same as the actuality appropriated in hearing the kerygma.

The former encounters all of the problems posed by the relationship between reflection and deity. Once reflection asks whether the words of the apostle are the words of God, no basis for answering in the affirmative can be given. It is possible to aver that Jesus speaks "as only God can" only as long as the truth of the assertion does not come into question. If it does, the experience of truth is beyond recovery because of the way in which the question engages reflection and dispels the religious assertion.

The theological declaration of the "death of God" can be understood as telling the event when the prophetic or reflective emerges from the religious (in this sense of religion). The theme of the death of God can be traced back at least to the sixteenth century. Luther had granted that it is correct to call it the "death of God" when the man "who is one thing or one person with God" dies, although God "in his nature (*Natur*)" cannot die (*WA*, 50, 590, 19; Ueltzen, " 'Gott,' " p. 565). In 1641 "God is dead"— "O Not!/Gott selbst liegt tot"—appeared in the second stanza of "O Traurigkeit, O Herzeleid," a Good Friday choral by Johann Rist, and after some vicissitudes (as Ueltzen shows) it was taken up by Hegel in his "speculative Good Friday" ("Glauben und Wissen," p. 432); it became the title of a theological movement in the 1960s with enduring consequences (see Jäger, *Gott*). The event to which it refers in the first place is the death of Jesus. What it declares is that the one taken by the disciples to be God has died and therein shows the truth of the divinity of God himself. But this is also a declaration of the moment at which reflection emerges out of religion, as the recognition is made that no one, not even the one taken to be God in the flesh, is God.

The formulation of this event as the death of God indicates that this emergence of the critical out of the religious is not a superimposition of something alien upon religion. Instead, it is the self-transcendence of religion, the gospel appearing in the death of God. "Thereby out of love he gained heaven for us," Rist's stanza affirms of the God lying dead. The ascertainment, made repeatedly by reflection, that no one and nothing is God because no one and nothing possesses divine properties coincides with the recognition made by religion when the appearing God is the victim of death. The religious relation comes to an end in reflection, that is true; but the termination can fulfill the religious relation when it is a movement within religion itself. Death takes away the appearing God, but at the same time manifests the deity of God. For the way in which the true God appears in the world as an object of experience is as other than one who possesses divine properties. The atheism of reflection is simultaneously the gospel in religion and the beginning of the experience of the truth of God as such.

That God exists can never be seen to be true. This conclusion seems to contradict the position taken by Pannenberg when he bases his theology upon the historical occurrence of the resurrection of Jesus. For he explicates that position, at least in part, by reference to the identification of Jesus with God. In *Jesus—God and Man*, the English title for his *Grundzüge der Christologie*, he calls it a central theme of christology to understand "how this man [Jesus] is God" (p. 31). Admittedly, the more frequent phrasing is that "Jesus is the Christ of God" and "In this man God is revealed" (p. 30); and this wording corresponds more closely with the actual undertaking in that Pannenberg's purpose is less to show that the predicate of deity can be seen as applicable to Jesus ("Jesus is God") than to show that in this man God shows himself as God. This is to say that, in the divisions offered here, what Pannenberg is arguing is not that Jesus is God but that God is God as the man Jesus. Nevertheless, the circumstance that he uses both wordings to make the statement indicates that he does not treat those two readings of "God is" as different, and therefore he can assume that if God shows himself, or is revealed, as truly God in the man Jesus, this is the same as demonstrating that Jesus is God.

Although this argument does not address by name the question of whether there is anyone who is God, since it has to do rather with the question of which among the many gods is truly God, it does fit into the framework set by the first reading of

"God is," as meaning there is one that is God. For there is a matter of verification at stake in Pannenberg's theology. The question of the reality of God is not whether someone appears, or is appealed to, as God but rather whether any of those who do so appear and are so invoked are truly God. This is the question of whether the implicit assertion made by faith is true. Consequently, the question behind the christological argument may indeed by formulated as this one: "Was the one whom Jesus addressed as his father real? And was that same one not only a real power but also the ultimate power—the 'power determining all of reality'? In short, was it God?" The test of this possibility is provided by the death and resurrection of Jesus. If Jesus was raised from death, then that power which Jesus named Father not only existed but was also recognizable as identical with God himself. God exists, there is one that is truly God, if there is a power that transcends the power of death. That there is such a power is what is shown by the resurrection of Jesus.

It is in this sense that Pannenberg's christological argument is an argument for the existence of God and intends to verify the assertion that there is someone that is indeed God. That one is identified as the one to whom Jesus entrusted himself and called his father. He is pointed out only by being so named and indicated. He has the attributes of God if he has power over all things, if there is no power greater than his. The test of such power is not to line up an infinite number of things to do in order to see whether he can do them; it is, rather, to ascertain whether he can demonstrate a power superior to the power that we experience as absolute, the power of death.

That death is an absolute power is a matter of experience. All things come to an end, and dying is the last act that we can ascribe to ourselves in the first person as "I." In the end " 'I' die." If the power of death is the greatest power there is, then we conclude that God does not exist—there is no one that has power over the ultimate power we experience, and the one whom Jesus called his father was not truly God. Pannenberg's argument is directed toward showing that there is such a power; the resurrection of Jesus simultaneously shows that there is one who is God and this one is the father of Jesus. Theoretically the argument could even be extended. If there were another case besides that of Jesus in which someone had been able to deliver from death the one who trusted him, then this one would be the same as the one that Jesus addressed as his father.

Since, however, there is a difference both in the content of the assertion and in the process of verification if we are dealing with the assertion that God is God as Jesus ("God is Jesus" instead of "Jesus is God"), Pannenberg's argument would not show that Jesus is God even when, or if, it did show that in the person and career of Jesus a demonstration of who is the true God is provided—namely, the one Jesus called his father, to whom he commended himself in his death, and who then delivered him from the death into which he had been committed. That one was, in Pannenberg's argument, truly God because he demonstrated himself as more powerful than the last power with which creatures have to contend, the power of death. About the God of Moses, by comparison, it was not yet clear that this was truly God, for Yahweh, who was capable of delivering the Israelites from their Egyptian bondage, might prove incapable of delivering his servant from bondage to death. Only the one who has power over death, or the one who is the end of the end, is truly God.

Can this whole argument, based historically, show that at least in principle reflection is capable of determining whether there is someone that is God, by the criterion that, if God exists, then death is not the last end; and death is not the last if a resurrection has actually already occurred? If so, this contradicts the conclusion that reflection denies an existent deity.

But Pannenberg's argument is impossible to carry out because it cannot overcome a fundamental difficulty. It cannot answer whether the definition of God as the power determining all reality is an adequate definition. It cannot overcome the circumstance that equating the meaning of "God" with the meaning of "power that determines all reality" is not an act of the deity itself. Reflection has no means at its disposal to show that the definition of God as the all-determining power is not an arbitrary definition of the word "God" but God's definition of himself. Conceivably reflection might determine whether there is "a power determining all reality" by the criterion of whether someone was resurrected from death—the selfsame person can say "I died and was raised so that I can no longer die" —but it could never determine whether this determination in turn is the work of God and not solely that of reflection.

In short, the defeat of efforts to show that someone or something is God originates not with the details of particular arguments, but with the circumstance that reflection cannot find a position from which to make such a judgment. If one judges, reflectively, that one's own judgment is a being judged by the one about whom it is a judgment (namely, God), it is nonetheless still reflection that is making this judgment about its own judgment. Reflection cannot recover what was lost in the transition from unreflective religion. If the recovery is to be made, it must take place by a power in religion itself to transcend unreflective certitude and to join with reflection. That is to say, the truth about God appears to reflection as the recognition that no one and nothing is God. But this recognition coincides with the end result of the prophetic principle in religion. It can be stated in the language of reflection—"we can never ascertain that something possesses the properties of divinity because our very effort to do so makes a positive conclusion impossible"—but it can also be stated in the language of religion as the death of God.

Furthermore, this conclusion about reflection and divine existence is not altered when theology is referred to a more original language, such as that of prayer. In his recent *Dogmatik* Ebeling does this by taking the "speech-event" of prayer as the model for making predications about God and as a hermeneutical key for interpreting theological statements; for the predicates of God are to be found, he says, in the things for which one prays. In prayer the supplicant inserts the reality of his own life into the same sentence as that which speaks of God. Any and all realities of the world that are of concern belong into prayer: "The language of the world that streams like a flood into prayer is reworked into the language of faith in the confrontation with God" (*Dogmatik*, I, p. 210). Translating the statements of dogmatics back into utterances of prayer is one way of understanding what they mean. But more than that, Ebeling argues, the very meaningfulness of prayer implies the existence of God: "If there weren't God, prayer would be senseless; even the mere interjection 'O God' implies that there is a vis-à-vis there that perceives something and also undertakes something" (p. 213).

All of this may be so, but the difficulty comes when the implication of prayer is to be elevated to a true judgment about prayer. Praying may imply that someone is there to whom one is praying, for otherwise the act would not make any sense at all and would not be distinguishable from a conversation with oneself. If reflection questions the sense of praying, however, then the reference to prayer evades the question instead of answering it. Whatever legitimacy a dogmatics based on the language of prayer might have on its own, it cannot undo the possibility of illusion that reflection raises. With respect to the language of prayer reflection has the same task as with respect to the whole religious relation. Can it recover by reflective means, and in the basic form of judgment, the content which is there in a living manner in religion and the speech of prayer? That praying actually takes place (the "speech-event" of prayer) cannot provide the model for making predications about God unless one can show how judgment, the thought-form of reflection, can recover what content is there in prayer prior to the critical question.

This is confirmed by the way in which the relation of faith to unfaith is left unreflected in the dogmatic system. Like Schleiermacher and others who have construed theology as an interpretation of original religious utterances, whether they have the character of expression or confession or prayer, Ebeling cannot incorporate the phenomenon of unfaith in theology. Faith is, Ebeling notes, "indubitably a given," "incontestably a datum," at least as a "religious phenomenon" (p. 79). But the

same could be said about unfaith. And if it is the experience of
the truth of theology that is at issue, then appealing to the one
phenomenon and not to the other is the same as evading the
question involved. For to remark that prayer, which without
doubt does go on, makes sense to those who are engaged in it is
not equivalent to showing that the sense and reality were not
illusory once the indubitable has become dubitable, nor is it, of
course, a way of deciding between the trusting and the suspicious
interpretations of these phenomena.

That the indubitable can become dubitable here is poignantly
shown in what is recounted of the aged monk Serapion by John
Cassian in his *Conferences*. Having been convinced by the deacon
Photinus, who instructed the group of monks on the immensity,
the incomprehensibility, the invisibility, and the like, of God,
Serapion found that, when subsequently called upon to pray, he
could no longer do so. "Heu me miserum! tulerunt a me deum
meum, et quem nunc teneam non habeo vel quem adorem aut
interpellam iam nescio," "Alas for me! They have taken my God
from me, and now I have none to hold, and I no longer know
whom to adore or to address" (*Conf.*, X; p. 77).

Aletheia of the One

For the second reading of "God is," according to which this
assertion is understood to designate and disclose the event that
underlies and occurs with all events, the results are different.
The experience of truth is related to two aspects here: whether
theological language manifests the one in the many, and which
events, if any, disclose the be-ing of the one who is. The language
of "God is" discloses the underlying subject of be-ing and enables
us to tell of the universal event to the extent that speaking
theologically, that is to say, ascribing actions to one subject
("God") and resolving the many actions into one action ("is") can
draw us into its sphere in the way that playing a game can; and
this language enables us to tell the one underlying event to the
extent that what we understand it to be saying can be seen to
agree with what we perceive to be taking place in those signifi-

cant events which hold our attention, stay in memory, and awaken an interest in seeing more of the same.

A formalistic understanding of the truth of "God is" is possible when it is explained that these two words are to designate the unity of agent and action in all events. Equipped with this interpretation, anyone is able at least to place the words properly within a whole discourse. No one would make the mistake, for example, of thinking that "God is" refers to something going on separately from the goings-on of "It is raining," "The earth rotates," "I am," and the like. It is thus possible to understand the statement as a formulation even before understanding it as an expression.

At this stage it makes no difference at all whether the words chosen for the purpose are the subject and verb "God is" or some arbitrary linguistic signs such as "S aes." For the only sense they have is the formal one provided by the rule of usage implied in the interpretation. To such a formalistic understanding the words do not manifest the unity they designate; they only designate it by stipulation. We can assign this meaning to them without necessarily having seen any such event as they are said to designate. Of course, it may be true that we would not even think of assigning such a function to words if no one had ever experienced the phenomenon they formulate—if, for example, no Greek had experienced anything to which the response was "*theos estin*," "God is." But the condition that someone must have had more than a formal understanding in order for a given function even to have come to light does not require that anyone and everyone must repeat the experience before the formal meaning of a phrase can be learned and before the language can be correctly spoken. On the contrary, it is possible to learn how to use theological language without being able to attach more than a formal significance to the words. If this were not so, semiology would be indistinguishable from semantics.

In the course of using such language, however, it may happen that the words, which at first were purely formal signs, become transparent to other meanings that they carry. When this occurs, we not only understand how to use a language correctly but also understand meanings *in* the linguistic signs. Only then can controversies about the proper name of God arise. They are rooted in the discrepancy between what the word as a formal sign is to designate and the meaning it actually carries in use. Where there is only a formalistic understanding, such a discrepancy cannot be noticed at all. But the general experience with language is that the effort to confine a word to its purely formal meaning is defeated because, as soon as it is put to use and is sounded in a whole context of sounds, a word takes on (or discloses) meanings other than the formal ones; it cannot be artificially separated from the other acoustic figures in the whole language.

The present standing of the English words "God is" is not fully clear. In part they seem to lack all but a formal sense, with no power to reveal the one they designate. In part they seem to reveal something opposed to what they designate. A striking case in point is contained in what Wittgenstein—a man who had once renounced his family fortune (Bartley, *Wittgenstein*, pp. 45-46)—wrote in a foreword to his *Philosophische Bemerkungen* in 1930: "I would like to say, 'This book is written to the glory of God,' but today that would sound roguish, that is, it would not be correctly understood." Then he went on to state what those words should, but could not, say—that the book "is written in good will, and insofar as it is not so written, but out of vanity, etc., the author would like to see it condemned."

The sense that one will be misunderstood if one uses theological words is not unique to the German or English phrase "to the glory of God." It also applies to so basic a theological wording as "God is." One can state what the words should say even while admitting that it is difficult to hear them actually say it. "Our linguistic tradition is full of references to God," Ebeling wrote in 1966. "But what *we* are able to say in this respect is little or nothing. . . . In our day, it looks as if talk of God . . . is . . . a mere form of speech, a dead relic of the language of the past" (*G&W*, p. 3).

Yet it should not be overlooked that one still *recognizes* that the words are intended to say what they do not say, and also that no other words will actually say the same. There is a dialectic in this theological language which enables phrases to be misunderstood but also to be understood as misunderstood. The formal sense assigned to them, and perhaps the memory of what they once were capable of saying, conflict with the meanings they actually carry in use. This is their unclarity: They may have a formal sense or, if they have more, they conflict with themselves.

To the extent that the English words "God is" have only a formally correct sense it marks an event in the language as well as a linguistic fact with which theological thinking must reckon. For it signals that words which once had a certain signifying power have lost it. (The time designated by "once" may be a moment that is always past for reflection instead of an epoch of years ago; Wittgenstein's plaint could have been heard in centuries other than the twentieth. Augustine too had lamented the absence of truth in the empty sound of those who spoke to him of God "voce sola" [*Conf.*, ch. 3]. This would not alter the state of affairs for the present moment.) Whether the power of such language can be reinstated by interpretations, which clear away such false meanings as the equation of "God" with a mythological entity and of "is" with "exists," or whether different words must be employed to say what was once said by "God is," is not clear. There are some indications that publicly in American English the word "history" has assumed the theological function of the word "God"—when, for example, it is said that "history" will "judge" what we have been and have accomplished or failed to accomplish. The unsettledness of the experience of truth here lies in the discrepancy between the words ("God is") whose sense formally is to designate the theological event and those other words ("history," "the process of history") whose actual use assigns that role to them, and also the feeling that if theological words are used, they will be misunderstood.

In *God and Word* Ebeling acknowledges the ambiguity of the present situation, but suggests that nevertheless the word "God" cannot be dispensed with because it alone is capable of naming

the human situation. For it to do so, however, it must be interpreted with respect to the situation, and its use must be "authorized" by the "word of God" itself. "The word of 'God' requires the word of God, as the word of God requires the word
'God' " (p. 33). The meaning of the word "God" is determined by
the necessity of its use. It must be used because without it neither
the human situation nor that with which the Bible and preaching
have to do ("the word of God") can be clearly put into words.

To say that there is no substitute for the word "God," however,
is not the same as saying that the word can be readily used or that
it is sufficient to recite biblical language in order to break
through the hindrances of the present situation. For the speaking that is to break through it "must submit to the most stringent
guarantee of certainty" (p. 36). That it is true, or that it speaks of
reality, cannot be made dependent upon established authorities,
as might have been possible at a time when there were such.
Neither the Bible nor religious institutions are in a position today
to provide the authority for speaking of God. Instead, such
speaking must "secure for itself the recognition that it claims" (p.
36) by its capacity to express the human situation more convincingly than does a technical approach to the world. This is to say
that it is not enough to claim to speak of God in the name of God
and to establish that claim by reference to some already acknowl-
edged authority. The claim can be established, as a speaking of
God done in the name of God, when that speaking itself has such
authority because it is actually hearable as the word of God. This
means first that it must claim to be spoken in the name of God;
but it also means that that claim is warranted: "A thing is not
word of God simply because it claims to be so" (p. 40).

How is the claim to be verified? In reply to this question Ebeling first announces a caution. We cannot verify whether words
are really the word of God (whether, e.g., our saying "God is" is
justified because God himself says "I am") in the way that we
verify the veracity of a witness to a crime or the reliability of a
promise. What we must do instead is ask whether what claims to
be the word of God presents the reality of which it speaks. "God's

word is itself verification. It verifies itself by verifying man" (p. 40). By this is meant that God's word (or, more exactly, the claim of someone to be speaking of God in the name of God) brings to light something that is hidden in the "field of experience" into which it is spoken. The "field of experience" is made up of what is already known and spoken of in a familiar way. That we already have the word "tree" in our language, for example, indicates the way in which one object is known to us and put into words. But in this field of experience, or this "context," there is always something that has not been said or understood; and the function of the word of God—of speaking in the name of God—is to say it and make it understandable. The role that is to be played by those who claim to speak in the name of God when they speak of God is, then, to say something that discloses what is otherwise unsaid and not understood in the context. It exemplified this role when, after the first exposures of the devastation worked by the war in Vietnam, Peter Berger declared it was time for someone to say, "In the name of God, stop!" For what had not been said was the real power to halt.

When what has not yet been said or understood is thus spoken in the name of God, it is a word that changes the context by making present what had otherwise been hidden through silence. It changes the context, but whether it is true depends upon whether it does "rectify" or "verify" the context instead of violating it: "That which is spoken into the context and added to it must correspond to that which is already hidden in the context and which is now identified as such and thereby brought to light" (p. 41). The truth lies in a correspondence between what is said into the context through the meaning of the theological words and what was already there, though hidden because unspoken. That hidden dimension is the human situation. To speak of God in the name of God is to put into words and thereby bring to light what is always occurring in a person's being the human being he is: "The word of God verifies itself as *God's* word precisely by addressing man with a recognition of his basic situation as word situation, that is, with a recognition of the fact that man

as man is always one who is already being approached by God"
(p. 44). What is always occurring in the being of human being is
thus said in words which speak of God. For that reason the word
which is heard as coming not from the person who speaks it but
from the situation of human being itself is the word that con-
fronts us as the word of God.

This basic situation, in view of which the word "God" must be
used, can be analyzed as one in which we are called upon to be
the ones we are, to be identical with ourselves, but fail to do so,
and one in which we are called upon to put reality and the
mystery of reality into words. "God" names the one who calls and
to whom we are answerable. Every act and occurrence is an
expression of that situation, but its character is not always manifest, it is not "constantly exposed" (p. 37). For this reason not
every time is right for speaking of God. Indeed, as Ebeling notes,
"at least part of the reason for the disappearance of talk of God
lies in a not unjustified sense of shame which is sensitive towards
the trivializing of what is extraordinary and tremendous" (p. 37).
The right time to speak of God is that time when no other word
but "God" is capable of saying what the situation in reality is.

Similarly, the right time to say "God is" (the affirmation with
which we are dealing here) is when something happens that so
fully elicits attention, asks to be remembered, and invites further
inquiry that other words than "God is" are inadequate to say
what is happening. These are the events which connect all occurrences to the being of God. But the ambiguity of these words
today is that no events seem clearly to call them forth in order to
bespeak their memorable character. Perhaps the first landing on
the moon in 1969 was a public event that came close to doing so.
Other events that break through the familiar way of speaking
seem rather to elicit the statement "Evil is" than "God is."

But even at the time of those occasions which do call for the
response "God is" in order to tell what is happening in them,
there is an additional question to which Ebeling calls attention. It
is the question of authorization. That the word "God" requires
"the word of God" for its authorization may be paraphrased

thus: Requisite for being able to say "God" (or "God is") is that one have learned a theological language so that one knows how to speak in such a way as to place "God" and "is" in their right syntactical locations and can understand the sense in speaking thus. To say "God is" about the event that can also be told in the words "Man has landed on the moon" is only giving a verbal embellishment to the matter if the being of God does not have some sense on its own independent of the landing on the moon. Therein lies the reason for cultivating theological speaking, even when it must be done in small or private communities rather than in public.

That it is possible to learn to speak of God correctly and with sense independently of current events can be shown by a simple example. No one would have any difficulty in picturing in the mind the episode of Moses and the burning bush. Without regard to whether there were literally a bush that burned without burning up and a voice emanating from it, any reader or hearer of the narrative can form a picture of a man and a bush, of its burning but not burning up, and of hearing a voice coming from the bush. In the same fashion one can picture what it is to hear someone say, as Jesus is reported to have said, "I am the truth" and "Before Abraham was, I am." Cultivating this kind of theological speaking without concern for whether it makes reference to actual events is a means of giving sense to talk about God, and this sense is what can "authorize" saying "God is" in order to express the time that is the same as the time of some literal occurrence.

Two things come into play, then, in the use of theological language. One is the necessity to resort to speaking of God because no other words will say what is meant. The other is some already existing sense of what God-talk means. To put the two in terms of the word "God" and the "word of God," as Ebeling does, may still reflect too much of the Protestant formulation of the principle of Scripture in which the writings of the Bible are in a special sense the word of God. But this does not alter the matter. There must be an authorization for using theological language besides a felt need to do so. For Ebeling the "source of authorization" is not the documents of the Scriptures, for they are not in any fixed sense the word of God, but it is a source that can be indicated by the name "Yahweh" in the Old Testament and the name "Jesus" in the New.

This situation is not unlike that of such language as the "tennising of tennis." What authorizes saying "There tennis really tennised" of a particular game played between M and N is that, apart from this game, there is some other expression of what it means for tennis to tennis. This is provided by the formal rules of playing tennis, but also by previous tennis matches that serve as "classic" performances of the game. From them we get an idea of what the tennising of tennis in reality is, or of what the tennising of tennis signifies in reality. They provide the "authorization" to say of other games, when the occasion warrants it, "There tennis tennised." This is the point that the question of authority makes with respect to theological language. An event so memorable as to be expressible only by saying "There God really was! In all of our language there are no other words that can say what happened there" does of its own character elicit those words. But this response is "authorized" (and not merely a sign of our own ignorance of language) only when the meaning of God's being, which we acquire by the rules of how to speak of "God" and of "be-ing" and by remembering such classic events as the "I am who I am" of the burning bush, can be seen to be the same as the underlying event manifest at the same time as the particular occurrence. In the end "God is" is authorized by the "I am" spoken by God. But we determine whether the "I am" we might hear in the words of some person, or through some event that speaks to us, is spoken by God himself not by seeing who the speaker is (since the speaker in any case is not God) but by whether it does present the reality to which "God is" refers us. An event about which we say "God is" is one whose underlying character is that of presenting to us an "I am" on behalf of an "I" that is not the particular agent of the event or any other person or thing, but an "I" that is present as other than the particular subjects or agents which point to it. At this juncture, however, the assertion "God is" becomes that of "God is . . ."

When theological language in use actually manifests the meaning assigned to it, the first moment of the experience of truth, that of *aletheia,* is present. This manifestation is similar to what Gadamer calls the truth of play. When a game as specified by its rules is put into play, its capacity to draw players and spectators into its sphere and to elicit interest comes forth; it shows itself as the "subject" it is. If playing a game is nothing more than mechanically following rules, the truth of the game does not emerge. Those spectators who find a game neither interesting nor tedious but only a more or less correct observance of rules of play are in a situation similar to those who can understand "God is" and related theological language as only a formal language game. Even when they know the rules of play, they do not see more than formal significance because they are not drawn into it. They are able to follow the rules of speaking—the rule, for example, that "God is" is to be said in particular of events that are striking, memorable, and significative of more—but they do not find it interesting to speak in that way, and they do not find that the words actually tell an event in its universality. Today it is unclear whether the words "God is" can tell that event, partly because the critically minded do not speak this kind of language. Is the lack of willingness to do so a sign that such speaking has no capacity to interest? Or is it that, for the time being, there has been a large-scale forgetting of what such language might even mean? Ebeling suggests that theological language is in difficulty because "the basic situation of man" itself has been pushed into the background, "abandoned to silence" (*G&W*, p. 36). That may indeed be one reason why the truth of "God is" is not experientially settled.

If the first side of this question is whether the language "God is" has the power to manifest what it designates, the other side is whether there are events which reveal the be-ing of the one-who-is, the *est* of the *qui est*, by calling for two kinds of statements to tell of them, one of which is that "God is." The situation is analogous to that of a game. For example, every time that a tennis game is played, it is true that tennis is tennising. Thus the question is not, strictly speaking, *whether* tennis tennises but rather which particular occurrences disclose that event more than others. Similarly, with respect to being, the question is not *whether* God (the one-who-is) is, but rather which particular occurrences disclose that be-ing of God.

About particularly eventful tennis games one is likely to say, "That was really tennis." In effect these words make note of the tennising of tennis, and a more correct way of saying what is to be said is to use a phrasing on the order of "There tennis was really tennising," or, more correctly still, "Then (namely, in the playing of that game) tennis was really tennising." Truth in the experience involves the sameness of time in the difference in meanings and referents. The time of the particular game is the time of tennis itself. A tennis game which catches spectators' or players' attention, which is memorable and makes one want to recall it, and which makes one wish to see more of the same or another game like it is a tennis game that discloses what is meant by the event "tennis tennises," and it makes the call for two languages to tell the event—not only "M played N" but also "Tennis tennised" there.

We find out in the first place what the game of tennis is by being drawn into it as players or spectators (or, formally, by reading the rules of the game); similarly, we find out what the be-ing of God is by being drawn into the "game" of being (or, formally, by understanding the rules of the thinking of being). This is what enables us to say in the first place that whenever a game of tennis is played, tennis is tennising; and whenever anything is at all, God is be-ing. But some games disclose the tennising more than others, and some events of be-ing disclose be-ing more than others. These are the occurrences about which we say, "There (then) tennis was really tennising, God was really be-ing." It is these events which make the experience of truth in the narratives which tell of them more than formalistic. On this side of the matter too, however, the experience is ambiguous. Two illustrations may serve to support this conclusion.

No single series of occurrences in the twentieth century has so demanded a second language besides that of human agents, intentions, and actions as has the Holocaust. What happened cannot be adequately told by a narrative whose subjects are human beings, political forces, and national entities. Something "supranormal" occurred. But it is not clear what that second language can be. Some authors (Richard Rubenstein, for example) think it calls for the negation of theological language; that is to say, it does call for saying something about God, but what it calls for is that God was not there and perhaps is not at all.

A book by Philip Hallie, however, may give a better indication of the current standing of theological language. In the background of his *Lest Innocent Blood Be Shed* was the question of what meaning existence has at all if "the pattern of the strong crushing the weak kept repeating itself and repeating itself." If the repetition were unrelieved, "the lies I would have to tell my children in order to raise them in hope—which children need the way plants need sunlight—would make the burden unbearable" (Des Pres, "Goodness," p. 83). While looking through some documents on the Holocaust, Hallie came across a reference to Le Chambon in southern France, a village of some 700 people with 2000 peasants from the surrounding country which had successfully kept more than 2500 refugees, mostly Jews, from harm during the Nazi occupation. Impelled by an interest in what had happened and how it was possible, Hallie spent three years in that place, getting acquainted with the people and their spiritual leader, the Huguenot pastor André Trocmé, and seeking to record as well as to understand what had occurred there. "Redemption lies in remembering." In a review of the book, Terrence Des Pres, himself the author of a work on the Holocaust, remarks, "The thing that makes the story of this village supremely beautiful is simply that it happened. These events took place and therefore *demand place* in our view of the world" ("Goodness," p. 84, emphasis in text). Of himself Hallie says, "I needed this understanding in order to redeem myself—and possibly others—from the coercion of despair."

With this book, "conceived and written on a modest scale," Hallie "has restored to the word *goodness* its rightful moral beauty." So Des Pres observes in response to the rhetorical question "When was the last time anyone used that word in earnest, without irony, as anything more than a doubtful cliché?" (p. 86). Another aspect to the intentional modesty of the book's undertaking is indicated in the subtitle, "The Story of the Village of Le Chambon and How Goodness Happened There." "Goodness happened" says less than "God was." One has the impression that a more suitable wording for the basic story Hallie narrates and strove to understand is not only how goodness happened, but how "God was," there. Yet it is not clear that such a subtitle could have been used. "God was" might not have accomplished for the being of God what, in Des Pres's judgment, is accomplished for the beauty of goodness. Just this seems to betray the ambiguous status of language which speaks of the being of God. The good and the godly may still be confused with each other, but that is only one element of the situation. The other element is that an author who is a philosopher, or perhaps any author whose readership is the public, might feel that to use theological language would be misunderstood, as though, for example, the episode in Le Chambon were being presented as a theodicy.

The story of Le Chambon, as told by Hallie, clearly requires two different orders of narrative. At one level there is the story of how, under the leadership of the local pastor and his wife, the villagers voted to make their place a "city of refuge" and how they then, with financial aid from American Quakers, carried on, in a routine and unheroic fashion, their work of hiding refugees from the Vichy government and the surveillance of the Gestapo. That historical narrative calls forth a narrative of a second order, which is epitomized in the subtitle as "Goodness Happened." "Goodness" obviously names an agent in a dimension different from that of the names of the villagers. But even this second

narrative may call forth another under the title of "God was"—
the story of Le Chambon, how goodness happened, and when
God was, there.

The addition of this theological narrative remains problematic, however, to the degree that whether "God was" would actually bespeak the eternal event, to whose time the time of any
other event stands in correspondence, is unclear. In this sense
the contemporary experience of truth in "God is" remains unsettled. It accords with this situation that at the end of a semester-
long course on the theme "What is theology?" which he
moderated, Georg Picht noted how almost none of the fourteen
coparticipants undertook to answer the question of what the
word "God" even signified. Picht evaluated this outcome by reference to the current situation. "Today," he said, "theology finds
itself in a position where it can only be silent about God or at the
most recognize the physiognomy of the suffering God"
(*Theologie*, p. 504). Theology seems to be capable of doing only
one of two things—it can be silent about God or it can speak of
him only in traditional forms. Indeed, the *deus absconditus* has so
deeply hidden himself that the only honest way of still testifying
of him is to be silent. Picht draws the conclusion that one should
not try to disguise the situation by using "costumes" which no
one believes anymore because they are merely historical. Rather,
one should recognize that the theological task today faces the
obstacle of the unthinkable and unsayable, the *Nichts des Denkens*.
Today there is no theology in the full and only sense of that word
because it seems impossible to think or speak of God. The
technical-industrial revolution has destroyed history along with
nature. "Mankind has blocked its access to the experience of
God, but is simultaneously resolved not to admit this to itself" (p.
504), and theology participates in this general situation of consciousness.

A second illustration of this ambiguous character of theological language is provided by the quest for self-identity that is part
of contemporary consciousness. In the possibility of finding oneself was projected an event which might disclose what is univer-

sally taking place. But the truth of this activity of searching was obscured just because it was not tied to theological language. It was more than a matter of individual biography. Yet the nature of that universal could not be put into the words of the theological tradition. It was formulated as a search for self, the question of how I can be the one that I essentially am; it was not understood as an expression of the be-ing of God in everything that occurs. For that reason there remains a discrepancy between the publicity given to, and the interest aroused by, such searches and the privacy which is entailed in anyone's being the one he is. Why should it be a matter of public interest whether I find out who I am? What is the "more than private" that is manifested in the public interest aroused by the question of self-identity? The unclarity of the experience lies in whether "my" being who and what "I" am is an issue that, underneath, is the event of God's be-ing. It is uncertain whether in those cases where someone does find the lost self the discovery can be understood and narrated as the be-ing of God. Can one say of such occurrences, "There (then) God is be-ing"?

The New Testament parable of the prodigal son (Luke 15) has been understood throughout Christian theology as an event disclosing the being of God—the kingdom of God is like what happens in the prodigal son's wanderings and return home; the son's coming to himself, coming to be the son he was, was the particular event that disclosed the be-ing of God underlying it. Today, however, this connection is not so easily made. Telling what the kingdom of heaven is like is not connected with the search for identity. The experience of truth in "God is" remains, accordingly, ambiguous. By formal rules "God is" does tell the universality of the event; in actual use, the words do not clearly do so.

A notable effort to break through this ambiguity and make the being of God audible in the quest for meaning and identity is Thomas Altizer's *Self-Embodiment of God*, in which the themes of self-identity, the nature of language, and the being of God are intimately fused. "Ever increasingly," he writes, the quest for words in which to speak of God "is becoming a quest for language itself, and for a new language, a language whereby we can actually and fully speak" (p. 1). "To speak of God is finally to speak of speech itself . . . in that pure otherness which calls every identity out of itself" (p. 40). Though "overt" theological language may not be "speakable or hearable," still a theological language "which will speak by way of the voice or the voices of our own time" may be possible (p. 4). The "uniquely modern obstacles to speech" result from a breakdown "in meaning and identity in the modern world," since speech is "our primal mode of realizing identity and meaning" (p. 1), yet this situation is "analogous to the original situation or situations of biblical faith" (p. 2); and it is just this analogy which warrants a theology that is at once modern, biblical, and universal.

The identity that Altizer has in mind is initially that of religion, of which the "primal identity" is made clear by "the ways of silence" and which challenges theology to "maintain and establish the actuality of speech," and those of both silence and speech, which are united in theology (pp. 5-6). But in course it becomes clear that this is also the identity and meaning of the assertion "I am," as the "I am" of anyone and the "I AM" of the one over all, "das Seiende im Allgemeinen" and "das Seiende im Höchsten," as Heidegger put it ("Onto-theo-logical," pp. 70, 139).

"Who is the 'I' of 'I am I' or 'I am this one here'?" is the question of identity; and "What does it mean for 'me' to be the one that 'I' am?" is the question of meaning. The contemporary situation is one in which neither tradition nor one's own reflection seems capable of answering these two questions, or of permitting one to say who "I" am and what it means that I am such a one. Therein lies the obstacle to speaking at all. To the extent that we know who we are and what it means for us to be who we are, to that extent we are also able to speak and to hear others speaking. But to be able to speak that identity and meaning depends upon there being a theological language in which it can be expressed. Hence the quest for a language is at the same time a search for the event of what, in traditional theological terms, was expressed as the be-ing of God. In that I can speak, God is. That God is "somehow"—exactly how is what is obscure today—contains the possibility of knowing who I am and what it means to be so. "Somehow" the being of God is to our speaking as the tennising of tennis is to the playing of a tennis game by M and N.

In this situation Altizer sees silence as the temptation; insofar as the "way of silence" is the identity of religion, it is religion that provides the temptation for theology. This is a temptation—so one may read Altizer—in the Kierkegaardian sense: silence is tempting because it offers an appealing possibility at the risk of self-loss. To succumb to silence is to risk losing the identity altogether in another; but not to succumb is to risk losing it in something that is other than identity. It is like the Adamic temptation to freedom—to actualize it is to risk losing the self by losing the self's destiny, and not to actualize it is to risk losing the self by losing the capacity to decide and act on one's own. To be silent is to lose identity, and this risks meaning. The two are together as are freedom and destiny. Speech runs the risk that when everything is put into words, nothing is said; whereas silence runs the risk that when nothing is put into words, nothing is said either. Silence tempts by the prospect that it can say the fullness of what is to be said just because it is beyond the limit of speaking. It seems safer not even to try to say who "I" am or "God" is and what it means for each to be what it is. But "theology must simply disappear if silence, or the silence of silence, is the true end of speech" (p. 5).

The identity "I am I" (or, abstractly, "A is A"), of which one could also speak in Hegelian terms as pure being, is thus more than a matter of what phenomenological reductions of self-world relations disclose as the origin of activity. When we trace a noema, such as the judgment "This is a tree," back to its constituent factors, one of them is the subject from which the act of thought, the noesis, originates. This agent-subject is expressed as "I," and what "I" am is disclosed as the origin of the act. It begins to come into view when our expectation concerning an object is disappointed. The object, which I perceive as a tree, may show itself as a telephone pole when I get closer or see it in a better light. This disappointed expectation shifts attention from the object to myself as the perceiving body, as—in Ricoeur's words—"not only my openness onto the world" but also "the 'here from where' the thing is seen" (*FM*, p. 33). More generally put: The changing silhouettes of an object are traced back to the changing positions of my body, and these changing positions are traced back to the "initial position which is always the absolute 'here,' " constituted as "a point of view" when the diversity of operations in breaking up the silhouettes and positions is ascribed "to the identity of a subject pole . . . which is, as it were, behind the diversity of the flow. . . . Thus, the 'it is I who,' implied in all my intentional operations, makes the position of the body as a whole prevail in the constitution of the *here* over the position of its members. 'Here' is the origin from which *I* see, not the origin from which my eye sees" (pp. 34-35).

This retrocursion, which starts from the appearance of an object and moves to the changing appearances and from there to the changing positions of the body and finally to the subject "I" as the origin of all operations, is a means of disclosing the self. It is one way of answering the question "Who is the 'I' of 'I am this one here'?" which comes into view only as expressed in its acts and embodied in its works. Moreover, it is possible to answer the question of meaning in these same terms. For what it means for me to be the origin of the operations which constitute the object as an object is to be a creator of a world. Both identity and meaning can be disclosed to this extent without recourse to theological language. But the identity in meaning underlying even this level is what theological language seeks to make manifest. To make a connection with theological language is to show that the identity and meaning of the self as creator of a world is at the same time the occurrence of the being of God. In that I perceive, intend, and thereby establish the objectivity of the things of the world, God is. "God is" puts into words the unity of events underlying all the individual occurrences in which "I create."

Accordingly, to trace a subject that is a speaking person to the subject that is "voice" and then to the subject that is "otherness," "silence," and "God," as Altizer undertakes to do, involves a movement other than phenomenological reduction. It is a movement from plurality to unity, but it stays within the same category. Phenomenological reduction shows the unity of subject in a plurality of operations; the other movement has to do with the unity of subject in the plurality of subjects, and the unity of speech-event in the plurality of speakings. In other words, it has to do with disclosing the one event, formally designatable by the words "God is," in the event of speaking. The question of identity is not answered by showing the "I" of "I speak" through tracing a noema to its agent. It is answered by uncovering the subject-character of language itself with a view to showing who it is that speaks in all speaking and, finally, to showing what it is that universally is occurring when identity and meaning are contended for in language. This subject appears as the voices and the voice of the present time and, more deeply, as silence, though silence is other than itself when it is the subject of speaking. In the end, and in principle, the process of language, of speaking and hearing, is the self-embodying of God. What is taking place when voice speaks is that God embodies deity as other than itself: "The pronunciation of the name of God evokes a special presence . . . that can be called forth by no other act of speech" (p. 38). The ultimate identity of language is at the same time capable of being a particular act of language, the naming of God.

In some sense "God is" (and this is so even of "God is dead") does designate the event underlying the occurrence of speech. But it does so under an inversion—God as other than God is the subject of language. To show this connection Altizer employs an identity between God and silence. The connection is not arbitrary—nor does it need to be justified by reference to its antiquity. The word "silence" and the word "God" are similar in that each of them can name its referent only in an "exile" from it. To speak the word "silence" is to break the silence, and to name "God" is to end the pure identity of God as deity, as pure transcendence. "God is the name of absolute beginning . . . a name which we must name in speaking of the advent of speech," but it is a name that can be pronounced only on this side of the beginning "and only in that exile which this beginning releases and enacts" (p. 29). "Only speech about God makes otherness manifest as world, and as the world of actuality" (p. 31).

The beginning, or principle, which is to be uncovered as the underlying identity and meaning is not the "I" of "I am this one here" or of "I think this" but the beginning that is the subject of language itself, in the way that tennis is the subject which becomes manifest in the playing of the game; not the "I," but the *being* expressed in the identity "I am I" is to be uncovered. What becomes manifest in the naming of God is this absolute beginning (or, if one will, the absolute subject), but it is manifest in "exile" from itself. The naming of God, like the very process of speaking and hearing, differs from the playing of tennis insofar as the tennis which is manifest in an eventful game is manifest as tennis and not, as it were, in exile from itself. By contrast, God becomes manifest in language not as such but as other than God and thus as in exile from deity. But this exile appears as his own deed and is therefore still expressive of his being. Even in the case of the death of God what matters is not that there is a death but that it is God who undergoes it. This, incidentally, was always the accent in Altizer's theology. The center of attention was not the disappearance of a belief in transcendent deity but the act of God which is told in the words "God is dead." These words name not something that befalls God but something that God does. They express the be-ing of God, of the way in which God is. In *The Self-Embodiment of God* this theme is transmuted into the rise of language. Clearly accentuated is that God is the subject of the advent of speech and, further, that the occurrence is an absolute beginning, from which everything comes, and the final end, to

which it returns. This book does for hermeneutics what the
theology of the death of God does for nihilism—it interprets
language as God's being.

Like the word "silence," the phrase "God is" can disclose what
it names only by transforming it in the process. But this also says
something about the way in which language takes its own course.
Identity, as in the proposition "I am I," says everything and
nothing; in Hegelian terms, it expresses pure being which turns
out to be nothing. On the one hand any tautology says everything that can be said about its subject, but on the other hand it
says nothing about the subject because it incorporates no difference between the subject and predicate terms. It says everything
emptily, and therefore it says nothing. Yet everything in its fullness and nothing in its emptiness are precisely what cannot be
said; they are the actually unsayable. To speak at all is literally to
say less than everything and more than nothing. Hence the saying of "I am I" or "A is A," which says nothing in the form of
everything, must be unsaid. This unsaying takes place in the
hearing of "I AM," in the saying of "I am," and in the saying of "I
am" so that in it the silence of "I AM" is heard. When identity,
the being expressed in the tautology, thus silences itself, by its
unsaying, it says the silence; that is resurrection. The meaningless identity of "I am I" has become an identity whose fullness of
meaning is the silence that it actually puts into words.

In sum, the identity and meaning sought are the ground and
end of the be-ing of God: as a transcendent "I AM," which negates and judges the hearer—"the hearer who hears 'I AM' in
the voice of call [i.e., as the sound in the voice of speech itself]
does so only by way of the act of self-negation" (p. 47); as an
immanent "I am," which every different hearer is able to say on
his own; as "I am the door" and "The door is I" in which the
sheer openness that is the meaning of existence is enacted—the
door "opens to nowhere because its opening itself is all actual
identity, all self-identity, all 'I'" (p. 88); as "'I am the resurrection and the life' . . . only when speech and silence are united" (p.
91); and finally as an "It is finished" when what is heard is the

silence that is the plenitude of meaning in every identity. "I AM" is heard in every "I am" insofar as "the voice of resurrection is the voice of silence" (p. 93). "In the presence of this event we can say nothing. . . . 'It is finished' " (p. 96).

The ambiguity today of saying "God is," with which both Ebeling's *God and Word* and Altizer's *The Self-Embodiment of God* deal, can be seen, finally, not only in how that language is actually heard but also in the disposition, or basic attitude toward reality, that is expressed by theological language. It reappears in a comparison between the dispositions expressed in the two languages, that which speaks of the one and that which speaks of the many events. "A tree stands in the meadow," "the plant is growing," and the like are assertions about subjects and doings in a world of manifold events, and they are capable of being true or false. By comparison with them the truth of "God is" can be experienced if there is a visible correspondence between the disposition concerning being that is conveyed by the language of the many and that which is conveyed by the language of the one. What grants the full sense of the truth of the objective world (and sometimes leads to the use of "truth" as a synonym of "objective reality") is the givenness of perceptible material, which is what it is on its own regardless of who we are or how we feel about it and which constrains us to think so that our thinking of an object accords with what it is on its own. The disposition conveyed in the language which thus reflects reality is that of letting what is there be what it is, and of telling it as it is.

Measured by this test, "God is" (the language of the one) agrees, by virtue of its attitude, with the language of realistic narrative and reportorial accounts as well as of physical science; for in them there is a disposition to acknowledge what is so regardless of wishes and desires. Publicly this is the disposition that discourse strives to embody. But whether the disposition to let-be accords with the language of technology and of art is not so clear. What distinguishes technology from science is its will to alter what is there. To the extent that "God is" expresses a universal disposition to let happen what happens, it is at odds with the technological attitude. This situation, however, is not yet clear either. One does not yet know whether technology is the measure of science, so that the disposition of willing what is there to be other than what it is and of helping it to become other, or whether, to the contrary, science is the measure of technology, so that letting what is there be as it is there, is the appropriate attitude for the thinking and saying of being.

The contest between science and technology is today a rehearsal of the medieval dispute over the primacy of the intellect or the will. If technology represents a deeper thought of being than does science, then what a thing is is not to be gauged by how it is present but by how it is a source of storable energy and how it resists or permits transformation; more real than how things are given to our sensation and thought is how they provoke our will and yield to technology. For modern science the reality of a thing is its being a datum of sense perception and judgment; for technology reality is the power of change. Only when we understand how to change things do we understand them in their innermost being; for what defines the deeper being of things is their potentiality to be other than what they presently are: they really are what they can become under technological transformation.

To science a tree in its natural givenness is the really objective entity; for technology the tree as a source of energy is the reality, and its natural givenness is only its first appearance. Mathematical physics lies between these two conceptions. On the one hand, an understanding of things according to the mathematical laws defining their relations is more in accord with their inner being than is an understanding based on their sensible appearance; but on the other hand, just this mathematical understanding is what makes technological transformation possible from the inside of things—not only can stones be turned into hammers and axes, but chemical compositions can be altered so as to bring synthetic things into existence.

In the Western heritage of the understanding of being, "God is" has a meaning whose disposition accords with the scientific but not clearly with the technological conception; the experience of truth in this assertion is therefore as ambiguous as is the relation between science and technique.

The Symbol of God

Whereas "God is" in the first sense is reflectively false (since nothing is God) and in the second sense unclear (because of the unsettled relation between the semiological and the semantic and between science and technology), in the third sense (as equivalent to "God is G") it is ascertainably true—but ascertainably false as well. It divides reflection against itself and thereby obliges reflection to question its own competence.

In Christian theology "God is G" is concretely the assertion "God is Jesus of Nazareth," the sense of which is that in the man Jesus the essence of God is shown; God is God *as* this man, God "is around" *as* the man Jesus. Barth puts it strongly: "God is Jesus Christ and Jesus Christ is God" (*KD*, II/1, p. 358). As the symbol or logos of God Jesus shows not what or who God is (quiddity) but how, or as what, God is the God he is (essence). It is "here that he himself has given himself to be found" (*KD*, II/1, p. 359).

Measured by the experience that is at the root of christology, the assertion that God is Jesus appears true to reflection because the figure of Jesus calls forth a discourse about the man as well as a discourse about God, and because there is a correspondence between the expectation that is engendered by the language which speaks of the being of God and the question of meaning that is elicited by the figure of Jesus of Nazareth. But measured by the non– or extra-Christian experience the same assertion appears false. Reflection here, in one subject, and reflection there, in the other subject, are both reflection; but they represent a division of reflection against itself.

The truth of a symbolic assertion is determined first by whether different languages, or orders of discourse, express the same time in that both of them state the meaning and both of them show the reality of the symbol; and, second, by whether the same language expresses different times—the same words both produce the expectation about the symbol and also record the interest elicited by it. Thus, in the first instance, the truth of "God is Jesus," a symbolic assertion, is determined by whether two languages express the real meaning. The figure of Jesus expresses its donation to thought by drawing forth a dual statement, so that "God is this one" and "This one is a man" both state the meaning and reality of the figure. The second statement, it might be noted, is not, as in Barth, "This one is *God*"; for what is in this aspect of truth is two orders of discourse. That both of them convey the meaning and show the reality is based upon the capacity of the first referent (the direct referent of the language) to point, in turn, to another referent. When the figure of Jesus of Nazareth evokes the question "What does it all mean? What is the career of this person all about?" this question indicates that the figure has the capacity to point beyond its literal appearance to something else. The second referent is present through a second language, which speaks of God.

The New Testament account of Jesus is a language that has its own referent; it is about the man who bore this name and had this career. The account is experienced as historically true to the extent that what it says about the man accords with what we can ascertain about him by internal and external critique of the documents that narrate his career. But the figure that they thus mediate can provoke the question, not whether what the texts say is or was true, but what the meaning of that human career is. This is the point at which the Jesus who is the referent of the first account becomes the signifier of another referent; he becomes a "word" on his own, a sign that carries a meaning. The capacity to do so is not restricted to Jesus of the New Testament. In our century the Holocaust can, similarly, elicit the question of meaning; it is a spectacle which of itself provokes one to ask what it signifies. But in distinction from the figure of Jesus in the New Testament, the meaning of this event, and its second referent, has not yet been connected to God's being God. No one has been able to say God is God as the Holocaust.

As symbolic assertions both of these cases are analogous to one in which we might speak of a log lying at a fireplace. The appearance of the log, its dimensions, its weight, and the like can be described in a language about logs. It is the referent of that language. But the log may, in turn, become a sign with a meaning when it draws from us the question "But what does it mean that trees can be cut into logs, logs can lie at fireplaces and be used for fire?" Then it warrants a discourse about trees in addition to the discourse about logs.

The two discourses that are involved when speaking of a symbol are, first, that about "being as"—a tree is a tree as this log—and, second, that of "being"—this thing is a log. Both express the meaning and both show the self-same object. The same holds for the figure of Jesus as a symbol. "God is God as this one" and "This one is a man" are both made with respect to the same figure. The experience of truth is that both are called for by the meaning and the reality of this figure.

The second part of the verification has to do with whether the same language expresses a different time, or whether "God is (God as) this man" both produces an expectation at the time of the saying and registers an ascertainment at the time of appearing. The truth is a matter of whether God's being God as other than God makes sense of the career of Jesus; it does so if the same words can be used to express the expectation concerning the object and also the interest elicited by the object. What it means for God to be who God is, and what it means for Jesus' career to have run as it did, are both formulated in the proposition "God is this man." In these words the otherness that is the meaning of the being of God and the otherness that is the meaning of Jesus' being a man coincide. To see that is to experience their truth.

In propositions about mundane objects, understanding the meaning of an assertion (the sense carried by the words) enables us to project what is so, and ascertaining what is so is possible on the basis of how the thing, to which reference is made, manifests its being. The correspondence between projection and manifes-

tation is the more precise means for seeing the agreement between understanding and reality, and assertions are true when
the words which project the object are the same as those which
record how the object shows itself (as in Heidegger's example of
the crooked picture on the wall). With symbolic assertions there
is a similar pattern. Theological language ("God is Jesus")
arouses an *expectation*, and the symbol (the historical figure of
Jesus) evokes a corresponding question of meaning. We may call
this question of meaning the *interest* elicited by the figure, but
interest is to be understood here specifically as that which is
expressed in the question "What does this mean?" "Expectation"
and "interest" are, then, to the experience of truth in symbolic
assertions what "projection" and "manifestation" are to the same
experience in world-related assertions.

Thus the proposition "God is Jesus"—or, in Barth's wording,
"God is who he is in the deed of his revelation" (*KD*, II/1
§ 28)—creates an expectation that is referred to the person of
Jesus—just as "A tree is what it is as this log" refers an expectation to this log even though the subject of the proposition is a
tree.

To show this pattern in "God is Jesus" one may take a shortcut
through a long historical development. The prophetic and apostolic tradition of speaking about God is connected with the relation of divine grace to human fault—or, more generally, the
relation between the divine and the human. Thus, when God is
understood in the Anselmian formula as "that than which no
greater can be thought," this tradition engenders a certain expectation as to what will embody the greatness of God (as gra-
cious) in the world of human beings (as fallen); and the experience of the truth of "God is Jesus" lies in seeing that this expectation corresponds with the interest in meaning evoked by the
figure of Jesus. If Jesus is of interest precisely as a figure which
shows the reconciliation between the divine and the human in a
way than which no greater can be thought, then the expectation
and the interest agree with each other. That is to say, if what it
means for God to be God is to be other than God and in being

other than God to be reconciling, then we can understand the sense in Jesus' career; the meaning of the being of God is identical with the sense in the career of Jesus. Our expectation is defined by the meaning of God's being God, and our interest is elicited by the question of meaning in the career of Jesus. To see that the one corresponds to the other is to experience the truth of the assertion "God is Jesus."

Requisite for this experience of truth is that the figure of Jesus elicit a question of meaning ("What does all of this mean? What does his death mean?") and that this question of meaning be in agreement with the expectation created by the language about God ("God is God"). Then to say "I can understand why Jesus' career took the course it did because what it means for God to be God is to be other than God and thereby to be reconciling and showing his unsurpassable greatness" is to have experienced the truth of the assertion that God is the man Jesus; for it is to say that the same proposition states the meaning of God's being who God is and the meaning in Jesus' being the one he was.

There is a variation on this experience that should be noted here since it involves a seeing *sub contraria specie*, the nature of which can be clarified through Kierkegaard's portrait of the "knight of faith" in *Fear and Trembling*, the one who is in everyday form what Abraham was in heroic stature. After imagining the dinner awaiting him at home as calf's head with trimmings, and despite knowing that he does not have the wherewithal to buy the provisions for such a dinner, this knight arrives home to find that the dinner is not calf's head at all but something quite inferior. Nevertheless, he is not disappointed by the fare; for, in contrast to a "knight of infinite resignation," he is able not only to forgo anything but also, despite outward appearances, to get in truth what he has given up in fact. Not in fact, but in truth, the knight had calf's head for dinner because what he had imagined as calf's head and what he tasted as the dinner corresponded with each other; his expectation was "true" even when it was contrary to outward "fact." That is how this knight differs from the knight of infinite resignation, who, were he in the same circumstances, would indeed be able to resign himself to not having calf's head and to do so with the satisfaction that infinite resignation itself can provide. The knight of faith gets back, in a way that perpetually tantalized Kierkegaard, what he has resigned; the knight of infinite resignation is content with having resigned it.

The experience of faith in this story can be interpreted according to both aspects of truth. First, the truth involved is that the being manifested in the anticipation of a calf's head dinner (the meaning in an image) is the same as the being which manifests itself in the actual eating of whatever was served (the reality in a taste). Hence, about the fare on the table both assertions can be made: "A calf's head is this," and "This is a hash." (Kierkegaard does not tell us what was in fact served, but hash will do for an illustration.)

Second, from the point of view of the accord between expectations produced and interest evoked, one can see that for the knight of faith there is an agreement between what was expected and what was received. This is so because the same language ("Calf's head is this dinner") expresses what is anticipated and what is eaten. What it means to be calf's head in anticipation and what it means for a dinner to taste as it actually does are both stated by the same words. The expectation expressed in the image and the interest aroused by the taste of the food accord with each other, however dissimilar "in fact" or *in specie* a calf's head is to hash.

Doubtless this forces Kierkegaard's example beyond what he intended, but it is a picturesque illustration of how two different things might be manifestations of the same being, and hence of how expectation and interest might agree with each other despite the difference in objective appearances. One might even envisage the possibility that this knight of faith not only on one occasion but repeatedly discovers that what he anticipates in an image of dinner looks nothing like what appears on the table and yet what is on the table fulfills that image by satisfying the taste. Moreover, he might also discover that on an occasion when he was served calf's head in fact he would respond by thinking or saying that this was not what he had anticipated. In such circumstances, the being with which this gourmand has to do by means of his imagination, which projects it, and his taste, which ascertains it, is the same although in the imagination it looks like calf's head and on the plate it looks like hash.

The same inversion might apply to the relation between what is expected on the basis of assertions about God and the interest in meaning that is elicited by a symbol. From "God is Jesus" one might expect the man Jesus to evoke interest by a display of impressive power, if God is the omnipotent Lord. Only if Jesus were to do miracles would one ask about the meaning of his deeds. Instead he evokes interest in meaning by the powerlessness shown in his death; and, paradoxically, this accords with the expectation, though it does so by inverting the expectation. Omnipotence shows itself under its opposite—divine omnipotence in human death. If the same experience is continually repeated, the correspondence between expectation and interest continues to be paradoxical—"contrary to expectation," when expectation is regarded in isolation from the symbol to which it is referred—but not the less real. As long as reflection can see such a correspondence, truth is experienced. If, like the Kierkegaardian knight of faith, a person says in retrospect, "What I expected to be the power of God is fulfilled in the interest awakened by the powerlessness of Jesus," this too is the experience of the truth of the symbolic assertion "God is Jesus."

That two discourses continue to be warranted by the self-same historical figure of Jesus, whether directly or paradoxically, and that the expectation about God and the interest in Jesus continue to correspond to each other, either directly or paradoxically, is the continuing experience of truth. "God is Jesus" is true because this figure still actually warrants both a reference to the man and a reference to God. The one discourse ("This one is a man") tells what is spoken about, and the second ("*God* is this man") tells what it is all about. Moreover, the interest elicited by Jesus still can be seen actually to correspond to the expectation engen-

dered by speaking of God. The discourse about Jesus signifies
the man Jesus as its referent. That referent becomes a word, a
sign with meaning, when it signifies another (which appears in
the question of meaning). This other is the being of God, first
expressed as a condition of the possibility of meaning—"if what
it means for God to be God is . . . , then . . ."; and this possibility
is actual when the interest presented by the figure of Jesus corresponds to the expectation created by the theological words. On
the basis of this experience it is possible to say that the assertion is
true.

The "when" of Jesus' being a man is the same as the "when" of
God's being God, and the "as what" of the meaning of the proposition is the same as the "as what" of the reality of the symbol.
This is truth as the identity of time in the difference of subject
and the identity of essence in the difference of time. One might
add that, strictly speaking, the tense of the statement should be
the past—"God was Jesus," as Paul has it in his "God was in
Christ reconciling the world"; for truth as the identity of time in
the difference of subject comes into experience as already accomplished. This, however, does not change the picture; and for
purposes of clarity it is simpler to put the illustrative propositions
in the present tense.

What complicates the picture is that the very position of reflection also continues to produce, in other reflecting subjects, the
opposite experience. Along with the Christian experience of
truth there exists an equally authentic opposite experience. It is
without doubt so that there are people for whom the essence of
God is manifest in the figure of Jesus of Nazareth and that there
are others who see in him only another human being—a victim
of injustice, a deluded Messiah, a revolutionary, a prophet, and
the like. These latter find that the expectation which theological
language produces does not agree either directly or paradoxically with the response which the figure of Jesus evokes. Not God
or the "kingdom of heaven" is what it is all about, but the self-
deception of human hope or the victimization of the innocent
and naive. For that reason they must say that "God is Jesus" is
not true, and they must do so on precisely the same reflective

ground as those who say the opposite. In their experience Jesus does not symbolize, by making present as a second referent in his own being there, the being of God.

Reflection cannot dismiss such nay-sayers as "spiritually blind" or irrational or take them in as "anonymous" Christians; for there is no basis on which such judgments can be made. The notion of anonymous Christians is more generous than that of spiritual blindness. But even this idea is tainted by the implication that the Christian reading of the non-Christian experience understands it better than the non-Christians themselves. The question of how the two different sides of reflective experience are related to each other can be answered only if there is a vantage point from which the dividedness of this experience itself can be judged. Simply to declare that the Christian experience is true and the other false, or that the two are the same though the one is anonymous, or even to declare that both are false because they contradict each other—all of these are arbitrary declarations that at the decisive juncture forfeit the very experience of truth with which reflection is concerned. As far as reflection can see, one can only conclude that the answer to the truth of "God is Jesus" is clearly a double one. The assertion is ascertainably true and also ascertainably false, depending on the reflecting subject; both faith and nonfaith experience truth.

This conclusion seems to be refuted by Barth's proof of the existence of God, as provided in his study of Anselm. Indeed, initially Barth's concern may seem to be not with "God is *G*" but with "There is a God." Barth does say that Anselm's proof shows that, according to the testimony of his own revelation, God has the freedom to prove his existence within the reality that is distinct from him (*KD*, II/1, p. 2). It is possible to prove the existence of God when one recognizes that the proof as carried out is nothing other than a repetition of the self-proof of God. This, Barth holds, is the unique value of the proof that Anselm developed in his *Proslogion* (*KD*, II/1, p. 343). Anselm proved God's existence from the fact that God has proved himself, and continues to do so, by setting himself as the beginning beyond which thinking cannot go and with which all thinking must begin. Furthermore, Barth makes a point of the difference between showing that God is *in intellectu* and showing that he is *in re* and calls attention to the difference between what Anselm does in the *Proslogion* in comparison with the *Monologion*. In the *Proslogion* Anselm treats the question of the existence of God separately from that of his essence in order to show that the object so named is not only thought of as existing but also really exists (*F*, p. 86). All of this would seem to indicate that Barth understands the existence of God to mean that we can ascertain, or prove, that there is one who is God because he possesses the attributes of God.

In the course of Barth's analysis, however, it becomes clear that this is not the case. What is involved is, rather, a discussion of the truth of the assertion "God is that than which no greater can be thought" when the sense is understood as "God is God as that than which no greater can be thought." This makes it an example of "God is *G*." If we then probe Barth's interpretation of the proof, we shall be able to see how he raises once more the question of the difference between the referent of "God" and the whole structure of the thinking of being.

Barth provides the guideline for his interpretation of the proof when he distinguishes two planes of thinking in order to show that the proof of the existence of God cannot be carried out on a plane where we separate understanding the meaning of the assertion from the ascertainment of what is so. If we treat the Anselmian formula "God is *id quo majus cogitari nequit,* that than which no greater can be thought" as intending to say that we can first understand what the sentence means and then set about to determine whether there is anything corresponding to it, we are thinking on the plane of the fool, the *insipiens;* and this is just the plane on which God's existence cannot be proved.

The two planes that come into question here are, first, that at which one reflects just on the meaning of the words and, second, that at which the words are used in order to say how the reality shows itself. Heidegger's example, already used, of the assertion

"The picture on the wall is hanging crooked" will serve as an illustration here too. When, with our backs to the wall, we understand the meaning of the sentence, we are thinking at one plane—that of reflection on the sense of the words; when, facing the wall, we use the words of the same sentence in order to state how the object shows itself in reality, we are thinking on the second plane. In both cases the same words are used.

Barth sets out this difference by reference to Anselm's own description. Anselm states that it is one thing to think a reality (*res*) by thinking the vocable (*vox*) that signifies it; it is another thing to think a reality by understanding the very thing that the reality is—"aliter enim cogitatur res cum vox eam significans cogitatur, aliter cum id ipsum quod res est intelligitur" (*Prosl.*, I, 103,18). It is one thing to think of the crooked painting on the wall by thinking the words of the assertion about it; it is another thing to think of that painting by using these words to understand the thing one sees when looking at the wall. The one is a matter of understanding the words; the other is a matter of understanding things with the words. What is at issue, as Barth interprets these two planes, is that we follow the direction given to our thinking through the linguistic sign (the name of God); in this case we rethink (*nachdenken*), or reflect on, "the pregiven thought of the thing meant" (*F*, p. 156) in such a way that we do not divorce the word from the reality it permits us to understand. That is to say, we reflect on it in such a way as to rule out the possibility of doing what we do with respect to the assertion about the painting on the wall—first understand the meaning, and then ascertain the reality. If we do make such a separation in understanding "God is that than which no greater can be thought," the consequence is that we must speak of someone other than the one that is named in this formula. This is why Gaunilo, who speaks on behalf of the "fool," misses Anselm's argument. He does not see that the name *quo majus cogitari nequit* is not merely one vocable among others but "a revelatory word and the revealed and believed name of God" (p. 109). Anyone who hears and understands this name finds himself placed not merely before a vocable, the vocable "God," but before an actual prohibition, which presents thinking with a real boundary. Gaunilo, for his part, does not wish to be content with a proof that is based simply on the word "that than which no greater can be thought" and on hearing and understanding this word (p. 125). Anselm's presupposition is indeed a word, but not, as Gaunilo thinks, a mere word; it is a word of God which also reveals his existence, or, as Barth puts it with overtones of biblicism, it is a word of God in the context of his revelation (pp. 125-126).

The point Barth emphasizes is that the decisive presupposition, the identification between God and the name "that than which . . . ," is introduced simply as a declaration. *Dico*, I say; *audit*, the other listens. I declare "God is that than which no greater can be thought." Upon hearing this assertion, the other, even if he is an *insipiens* who denies the existence of God, cannot avoid thinking the meaning of the word himself: "God is the one who manifests himself in the prohibition against thinking anything greater than God" (p. 102). The name is an intelligible sound, and the prohibition expressed in it is clear in itself. Thus, anyone who agrees to interpret the vocable "God" through the name "that than which no greater can be thought" cannot complain later that the word "God" is meaningless.

The question, however, is not whether the word "God" is intelligible but whether it manifests the real existence of the one it names. In the *Proslogion* Anselm sets out to prove not only that God must be thought to exist, but that he also really exists. When an object is thought to be not only possible but also actual, then it is thought of as existing in some way—whether the mode be hypothetical, poetical, mendacious, or erroneous; but the thought of it as actual does not yet determine that existence really belongs to the object. Real existence must be thought, known, and proved independently of the *esse in intellectu* which accompanies the thought of the object. The question is whether that which is an object of thought is also something over against thought, or whether the object "steps out" (*ex-sistere*) from the

inner circle which contains the objects of understanding, the
circle of *esse in intellectu.*

But if the very separation between being in the understanding
and being in reality is to be ruled out by the name of God, how
can such a proof be carried out? The manner in which Barth
replies to this question in his interpretation of Anselm's proof
shows that what is involved in the proof is not the truth of the
assertion "There is a God" but the truth of the assertion "God is
truth, that is, the unity of thought and reality." In the phrasing
that has been used in the current discussion, the assertion is
"God is God as the unity of meaning and reality," where the
unity of meaning and reality refers to what is given in the words
"that than which no greater can be thought."

Barth likens the relations that come into play to three circles.
The innermost circle is that of being thought (*esse in intellectu*);
the next is that of being there (*esse in re*), or real existence as
compared with existence in the understanding; and the third is
being in truth, both in thought and reality. "That which is both
in the understanding and in reality is identical with the true" (p.
87); for just that reason the truth of an assertion depends on this
that it designates as really being something that really is. (Barth
makes reference to Anselm's *De veritate* 2,I,178,6 as a source for
this statement.) What is to be shown in the proof is that "the
object designated as God cannot be thought of as being only in
the understanding" (p. 89); that is the intention of the proof in
Proslogion 2-4. And, according to Barth, Anselm conducts this
proof as a proof of the existence of that one whose existence
alone can be proven. Only the existence of God, and not that of
any other, can be proved; other things can be known to exist but
cannot be proved to exist. God is different. Not only can his
existence be known; it, and it alone, is an existence that can be
proved.

How then does the proof proceed? Barth correctly notes what
most interpreters have overlooked: "God is that than which no
greater can be thought" is not intended to be a definition of the
nature of God, from which his existence is to be deduced. It is

not a determination of the character of God. Instead, it formulates a rule of thinking and nothing more. The significance of the proof lies in this that, starting with nothing more than the rule of thought contained in the name of God, one arrives at the conclusion that God exists not only in thought but also in reality. The rule states that if we can think of anything greater than the one we are calling God, then we are not thinking of God at all. According to this rule we can decide the following alternatives:

1a) God exists only in our mind and not in reality. That is to say, the word "God" has a meaning but there is no reality that corresponds to it.

1b) God exists both in our mind and in reality.

Since we can recognize that the God of (1b) is greater than that of (1a), we understand that we cannot think of God as only a word. If we do try to think of him thus, the consequence is that we are not really thinking of God, who is shown by the name *quo majus cogitari nequit.*

2a) God exists in reality as a matter of contingent fact.

2b) God exists in reality and could not exist.

Here again (2b) can be seen to be greater than (2a). A God who does exist at the present time and under present conditions, but could also not exist, is one than which a greater is thinkable (p. 136).

This sequence, as Barth sets it up, can be carried to the reflexive level in a third alternative.

3a) We think: "We must think of God as necessarily existing, yet even so, he may not really exist because our thinking may be deceptive about reality."

3b) We think: "We must think of God as necessarily existing, and he does also necessarily exist."

Since the one we think of in (3b) is greater than that in (3a), we cannot think (3a) without changing the object of our thought to someone other than the God who is *quo majus cogitari nequit.* What is proved thereby is that where God is declared and understood to be that than which no greater can be thought, God exists in the hearer's mind because the meaning of the name given in the predicate is intelligible; and, further, where God exists in the hearer's mind, he does not exist merely there, for such an existence would not be one than which nothing greater can be thought; and, finally, where he exists in the mind and reality, he cannot not exist. Whatever exists only in the mind cannot be known as God (p. 123).

Thus, whoever hears the name of God, "that than which no greater can be thought," cannot regard what it names as merely an intellectual entity and cannot even hypothetically reckon with the nonexistence of God. God, but only God, so exists that even the thought of the possibility of his nonexistence is impossible. This is the real barrier that is presented to thinking by the name of God. Anselm's proof shows that it is impossible even to form the thought "God may not exist" if God is understood as that than which no greater can be thought. One can, of course, say the words "God may not really exist," but one cannot form a thought grasping the meaning of those words, because the effort to do so leads to a contradiction.

This is, in brief, Barth's exposition of Anselm's argument. In the plain, ordinary words of the name "that than which no greater can be thought" the referent of the name is present. The words reveal their object; the one whom they name and show to the mind is present in the very words. There is indeed a distinction between the meaning of the words and the reality to which they refer and which they present. This distinction is pointed out when the rule of thought contained in the name is formulated as such. But the course of the proof shows that this distinction is what is overridden by the presence of the reality in the name. The name of God is a reality that is also a meaning, and a meaning that is also a reality. Thus, thinking the meaning of the words which give God's name is to the knowledge of God's existence what perceiving a physical object with the senses is to the knowledge of the existence of mundane objects.

The Anselmian proof does not compel anyone to agree that God is that than which no greater can be thought; this initial identification remains the declaration of faith and a presupposition of the proof. But it does show that, if anyone accepts that initial identification, then God's existence is known because he is really manifest in the words that are his name.

This would seem to say that there is at least one symbol which shows the being of God indubitably. "God is God as the word 'quo majus cogitari nequit' " seems to be demonstrably true and demonstrably not false. If so, this is an instance where "God is . . ." can only be experienced as true, and reflection is not divided in itself.

But this conclusion does not follow. While the proof, as Barth sets it out, does indeed show that it is impossible to think the nonexistence of the God so named and that it is impossible for that God not to exist, yet it stops before it reaches its end. For, in addition to the alternatives already named, there is another to be decided according to the rule of thought "Think the greater of God":

4a) God exists and cannot not exist.

4b) God is free to exist or not to exist.

This is not the choice between contingent and necessary existence, for it has to do with freedom and necessity. The same rule of thinking by which the other alternatives were decided can be applied here. Which is greater: God who must exist, or God who is free either to exist or not to exist? Which is greater: God who must be God and cannot be other than God, or God who can be God and can also be other than God? Again, (4b) is clearly greater than (4a). Hence, we do not have to think of God as existing in reality as well as in the understanding, and we do not have to think of him as existing in the understanding. The very rule of thought which, in the proof up to the point to which Barth takes it, shows that God cannot not exist and be understood to exist now shows a greater possibility. What is greater than the God who is that than which no greater can be thought is a God who is that as well as another. And what is greater than a God who cannot not exist is one who is free to exist or not to exist. The very proof that Barth employs does in the end lead to the same conclusion as the one drawn about "God is Jesus." It splits reflection in itself; for "God is that than which no greater can be thought" is demonstrably true and demonstrably false, for reflection here (in one person) and reflection there (in another person). In the end the name *quo majus cogitari nequit* is a symbol which shows where the essence of God is to be seen, but shows it under the double face of other symbols of the being of God.

The Anselmian proof will show that in the thought of "that than which no greater can be thought" we are presented with the unity of thinking and being. It does not show that God is that unity. Indeed, to identify God with it is to make a declaration of faith to the hearer—*dico, audit*. The proof may show that that than which no greater can be thought does exist; it does not show that God is that one. Must anyone who thinks of God think of the prohibition contained in this name? Barth himself asks that question, and he answers that God is so named because he has so revealed himself and because one believes him as he has revealed himself (p. 145). But it is obvious that not every one does so believe him and that the assertion "God is (God as) that than which no greater can be thought" can be experienced both as true and as not true.

If "God is that than which no greater can be thought" is intended to be a definition of terms and nothing more, then what it proves is that "that than which no greater can be thought" exists and the additional name of "God" serves no purpose. If on the other hand, the assertion is not meant as a tautology or a definition of terms, then it is noteworthy that the existence of Jupiter could be proved in exactly the same way. Should someone declare, "I believe Jupiter is that than which no greater can be thought," the truth of this declaration (or presupposition of faith) can be shown in equal measure. If an opponent contended that Jupiter does not really exist, this believer could reply, "But the Jupiter of whom you are speaking is not really Jupiter because we can think of a greater than he." The dictum "Jupiter is that than which no greater can be thought" places a barrier before our thinking just as much as does "God is that than which no greater can be thought."

The significance of Anselm's formulation is that it points out a place at which thinking cannot be separated from real being. *Quo majus cogitari nequit* is the pure thought of . . .; what it is the thought of is the nonseparability of thinking and being, or the point in thinking at which, of itself, it is open to what is other than thinking. Its sense is that of an idea which cannot be merely an idea, and thus it opens thought to the real referent of thinking.

If we then proceed to identify what is that than which no greater can be thought, we do not immediately come to God but to the structure of the thinking of being. We cannot think anything greater than the relation between the self and the world (the thinking of being) because all thinking is involved in such a relation. All thinking of being presupposes this structure and cannot possibly escape it. At the most we may name something greater as "nothing." But as soon as it is named, and we try to think of nothing, we subject it to the structure of the thinking of being. What we think is not nothing but something. In this way the structure of the thinking of being is that than which no greater can be thought, it is that which is both in our understanding and in reality; and it is therefore the immediate referent of the thought contained in the Anselmian phrase. To *think* that than which no greater can be thought is to be in the presence of the structure of being.

Accordingly, Barth's interpretation of Anselm's proof, which later became the basis of Barth's theological thought, is a variation on the identification between God and the whole structure of the thinking of being. It is a variation on the tautology "God is God," which can be interpreted as the assertion that God is God as the identity of thinking and being. That identity is given in one way in any vocable. The vocable "tree," for example, is a unity of thought and thing; as an acoustic or visual figure it can be physically perceived, but as carrying a meaning it must be apprehended as a thought. In another way that identity is the basic character of language as a whole, since reality and meaning are brought together in it. Thus the assertion that God is God as the unity of thinking and being can also be stated by saying that God is God as the word (either as the vocable "God" or as the whole of language). All such assertions, however, are intended to point out where, or as what, God is God; and they all divide reflection between those who can see the essence of God there and those who do not. This is not a division between the blind and the seeing, for it is a structural duality in reflective subjectivity itself.

With this concession reflection itself is jeopardized; the vantage point of *Dasein*, the *anima aeterna*, from which truth is experienced, seems to be located in untruth. Here *Dasein* loses itself; for in its concretion the "eternal soul" cannot come together with all being. This ultimate defeat stirs reflection to ask about its own essence and competence.

4

The Depth of Truth

In revelation we have to do with the gift of openness for the openness of God himself, that is, with the truth of truth itself.
—Karl Barth, *KD*, I/1, p. 73

The Christ is Jesus and the negation of Jesus.
—Paul Tillich, *BR*, p. 85

To what does reflection turn for illumination concerning its own essence and competence? What is the truth about the truth that is the object of reflective thinking? As the identity of being in the difference between meaning and reality, truth is a reflective object, a phenomenon, differing from logical objects and sensational ones. It is experienced in assertions and on objects when one sees that what is said or thought is the same as what is so.[1] With reference to the basic theological assertion "God is," the experience varies with the three senses that can be understood in the words. As asserting the existence of something or someone godly, "God is" is experienced as false; as asserting and manifesting the unity of event in all events, it is experienced ambiguously; and as indicating where the essence of God appears, it is experienced as both true and false.

This last result jeopardizes reflection itself, by splitting it into two incompatible parts. Reflection is the standpoint from which the true is distinguished from the false. But here this very reflection collapses the distinction, which is to say, it seems incapable of seeing where the true and the false appear. For light on its own status reflection must turn to reflexivity, a reflection on reflection. If that to which reflective thinking is turned is the

153

phenomenon that appears in the relation between meaning (understanding, *intellectus*) and reality (apprehension, *res*), then the relation between reflection and that phenomenon is, in turn, the concern of reflexivity.

To have a definite picture of where reflexive thought fits, it will be helpful to recall three of the four paradigms introduced in the first chapter:

(1) "This is a tree" is a paradigm for the thought of a mundane object, in which being (the "is" of the proposition) is presented in the synthesis of percept and notion, singular and universal. It relates an intuition to a notion.

(3) " 'This is a tree' is true" is a paradigm of reflective thought, in which being is presented in the synthesis of meaning and reality, or the synthesis of time in language. It relates an understanding to an apprehension.

(4) " ' "This . . . " is true' is true" is a paradigm of reflexive thought, in which the depth of being is presented in the synthesis of the phenomenon and its reduplication. It relates a phenomenon (truth) to itself.

Mundane, or literal, thought has to do with the experience of sensational or logical objects; reflective thought, with the experience of reflective objects, or phenomena. Reflexive thought is concerned with the experience of depths, that is, of the self-transcendence or self-duplication indicated in such phrasings as "the truth about truth" and "the goodness about goodness."

An attentive reader will want to ask whether the progression can be carried further. To this there are two answers. First, the experience of the depth of truth cannot be carried further, but only repeated indefinitely, insofar as the "depth of the depth of truth" has a content no different from the depth of truth. There is an intentional difference between "truth" and "the truth about truth," but there is only a verbal difference between "the truth about truth" and "the truth about the truth about truth." Second, the movement from prethought to reflexive thought completes the course of thinking. Thinking does, indeed, have one thing left to do; and that is to invert itself, so that *noein* becomes *metanoein*, thinking becomes afterthinking. The possibility of this turn lies formally in the freedom of thought: one can think of thinking *as* thinking, but one can also think of it as other than itself—as the being of God. The freedom to make this inversion is the source of creativity. A woodsman would not get firewood, to say nothing of furniture, out of a tree if he were not capable of thinking of the appearing object as other than how it appears. When applied to the whole process of thinking, this same freedom is the capacity to turn thought into afterthought. What is other than our thinking is, normally, the other's being. Hence the move to *metanoein* is to think of our thinking of being as the being of God for our thinking. More particularly, in the present context, this would mean that one can think of our experiencing truth (seeing identity in difference) as God's being different from himself, and of our experiencing untruth as God's being at one with himself. To do so is to form a thought that represents the transition from thinking to afterthinking, or what is theological thinking in its most proper sense. To take this step, however, lies beyond the scope of the present study. Its possibility is indicated here only for the sake of completeness.

One step short of afterthinking is reflexivity, which completes the course of thought. It is this last, reflexive plane of thought to which the reflective experience of truth has now led. As truth splits into meaning and reality, when it appears on the plane of world-related thinking, so the depth of truth appears as the true and as the untrue when it appears upon the plane of reflective thinking. Truth appears upon a reality in correlation with a meaning; the depth of truth appears upon the true in correlation with its other, the untrue.

The objects of reflexive thought can be designated with the same words as those of reflection. Thus, about truth as the object of reflection, it can be asked, "What is the truth about truth?" This wording indicates the kind of reduplication that reflexivity involves. It is a reflection on reflection, and its objects are the objects about objects. If the objects of reflection are named as truth, beauty, goodness, identity, value, right, and so on, the objects correlative to reflexivity are the truth about truth, the beauty about beauty, and so on.

The issue with which reflexivity is concerned is whether a divided reflection has a phenomenon correlative to it. The split, which seems to defeat reflection as a standpoint from which to see truth, takes on a different character when it is seen as a response to a reality that can be apprehended only through such a split. For then the self-defeat of reflection is the experience of the truth about truth, or the depth of truth. Reflexivity synthesizes the true and the untrue in the depth of truth, as reflection synthesizes meaning and reality in the phenomenon of truth. Reflection sees that in the experience of mundane objects being is split between meaning and reality—the "is" of the proposition and the "is" of the object. The wholeness of being is recovered in the experience of truth as a synthesis of meaning and reality. Reflexivity sees that, in the experience of the phenomenon of truth, being is divided between the true and the untrue, and it synthesizes the two in the experience of the depth of truth. In the presence of the depth of truth, the experience of truth is also relativized. That is to say, to experience the truth about truth is to see truth as originating in a depth from which both the true and the untrue emerge. This *is* an experience of truth, because there is a correspondence between the reality presented, and the meaning understood, as the depth of truth. But the very experience includes a reference to both the true and the untrue. The real depth of truth is the sameness in the difference between the true and the untrue, which is co-presented with the reflective reality of truth in the same way that reflective realities are copresented with mundane objects. As the object "truth" is given not to sensation and understanding, but to reflection, in the relation between the meaning and the physical reality that, for example, "This is a tree" bespeaks, so the depth of truth is given not to reflection, but to reflexivity, in the relation of the true and the untrue.

To what does thinking turn in order to see this? To think literally of mundane objects we turn our attention to percepts and notions of things; to think reflectively of phenomena we turn our attention to meaning and realities in relation. To what do we turn in order to think reflexively?

Phenomenology of Language

The first answer, which in its modern form came at the end of idealism and of which Daub's "Über den Logos" provides a document, is that such depth-objects present themselves in language itself, when words are simultaneously the carrier of meaning and the donation of reality. One can see how this suggestion arises. In prethought, as we know it through recalling dream-states, no distinction is made between thinking and being, subject and object. Making that distinction is the work of mundane thought—the literal thinking of objects by conscious subjects. Prereflective literal thought, in turn, makes no distinction between reality and truth; things are what they appear to be, and the truth of matters is exactly the same as their self-presentation. At this prereflective stage the experience of truth is not identified as such; for truth, reality, and meaning are fused. With the emergence of reflection, the true is distinguished from the intelligible and the real because it is seen as the identity of being in the difference between meaning and reality. This is registered in the medium of language by the circumstance that the same words can be used to show the object to mind at one time in a meaning (as when, with back to wall, one says "The painting on the wall is crooked") and to the mind at another time in a reality (as when, facing the wall, one says the same). This state of matters is circumscribed by the phrase "the identity of substance in the difference in time." The other mode of experiencing truth, which was involved in the second and third readings of "God is," is that of an identity of time in a difference of subject, as illustrated by events whose meaning and reality warrant two languages, discourses about two different subjects.

When the same language will both present a thing in a meaning and also interpret the thing as it shows itself in reality, the experience of truth is embodied in the sameness of language and the difference of time. With respect to the metaphysical world, this pattern substituted the necessity of thinking for the self-presentation of a sense-object. The difference in time then was marked by the possibility and the necessity of a thought. That the same assertion could express a meaning, as a possible thought, and also show a constraint, as a necessary thought, reconstituted the experience of truth—the correspondence between the freedom and the necessity of thinking as embodied in the self-same language—upon metaphysical objects. As was noted earlier, however, metaphysical objects become dubious when it is seen that the necessity of thought, which arises from within thinking, is not the same as the constraint of thought imposed by what is other than thinking.

It is at this point that the suggestion of a reflection on language itself arises. For, on the one hand, language embodies thought in a sound and a sight, thereby becoming more than pure thinking; on the other hand, it is an interpretation of being, and therefore more than a mute datum. A word is a thought and a thing simultaneously. As an acoustic or visual figure it can be physically perceived; as a carrier of meaning, it is a thought capable of guiding or shaping the thought of the one who undertakes to understand it—the word "tree" makes one think of a tree. If a word is a thought-thing, a unity of meaning and reality, the possibility suggests itself that some words or propositions may be so constituted that they present being both as meaning and as reality at the same time. The truth of such propositions would have to do with their capacity to project a meaning as well as to donate, and not merely interpret, a reality. In mundane experience reality is found in an appearance to sense perception as interpreted in the language which shows it. But if there are words or propositions which can simultaneously project and present the being of which they speak, then on the one hand no additional reference to a sense object is required for the experience of truth, and, on the other hand, what shapes thinking is not the necessity of thought laid down in the rules of clear and consistent thinking, but the constraint upon thought that language itself presents.

This was the possibility that Daub took advantage of in his essay "Über den Logos: Ein Beitrag zur Logik der göttlichen Namen," probably the first essay in modern theological semantics though not designated as such. It is an effort to carry out a theological reflection in which the real object of thought is not a sense object or a logical object, but the word or words themselves. Daub seemed to be aware of the innovation when, at the end of the essay, he remarked that it is also the question of the origin of language that is involved in the theological reflection, a question whose answer is a task deserving the attention of an academy of sciences. This not to say, of course, that the quest for a language which is simultaneously conceptual and donative, reflective and responsive, abstractly correct and symbolically real is uniquely modern; it is an enduring strand in the history of thought. Augustine's invocation "O veritas, veritas!" as against the empty sounds of speech about God is on the same order, just as his *Principia Dialecticae* already identified the elements of modern semantic theory by distinguishing *verbum* (the sign), *dicibile* (the sense), *dictio* (the unity of sign and sense in the use of words), *res* (the referent) and *vis* (the import, or capacity of a word to hold good, *id quo cognoscitur quantum valeat*). But the distinctiveness of reflection on language comes out only in the modern period, and for this period Daub's essay is a forerunner. Hegel's notion of a "concrete concept" tends in the same direction, of course; for a concept that is concrete is in effect a concept incorporated into a word in such a way that the word is simultaneously the carrier of the abstract thought and the donation of the reality. The concrete concept of "God" is nothing other than the *word* "God" when that very word expresses the idea and presents the referent it signifies.

Daub's contention in this matter is that "egoistic" reflection, in which "I" am the position from which judgments are made and the source of the thinking, is transcended when it becomes a reflection on language. Daub still calls it "speculation," though this is inaccurate insofar as speculation has to do with ideas and with words only as their carriers. The problem with which this kind of thinking must deal for the experience of truth is that of distinguishing between the time of the meaning and the time of the reality. With sense objects the two times are kept distinct by the engagement of sensation in the whole experience. With objects that appear in language the two times can be kept distinct in an artificial, chronological sense: one can treat the words at moment t as carrying a meaning to be understood and at moment $t + 1$ as presenting a reality. But this distinction is the work of the reflecting subject; it is not rooted in the being that gives itself now as meaning and now as reality.

This problem can be circumvented, however, in the case of words which, independently of how one might choose to regard them, do at times only convey a meaning and at other times present a reality. For then the distinction between the projection and the donation, the meaning and the reality, is in the being of language rather than in the thinking subject. At any time whatsoever one can understand, e.g., the proposition "God is that than which no greater can be thought," but only on certain occasions do the words also take on the capacity to present the reality of the being of God, that is, the synthesis between the name "God" and the name "that than which. . . ." Again, one can think the meaning of "God" as "not-I" at any time; but whether there is any reality corresponding to it depends upon the capacity of the word on at least one occasion to *be* the not-I for which the name stands. This indeed seems to be the view Daub sets forth in his essay, which is admittedly cryptic—he had long before decided to incorporate the *Anstrengung des Begriffs* into his writing so as to ward off the facile criticisms of the day.

The essay deals with the identity between God and the word, in the triple sense of the word "God," the word as language (*logos*, discourse), and the word as the Bible. This identity is stated in the compound proposition "God is the word and the word is God." The difficulty of understanding such a proposition is, according to Daub's analysis, that it breaks with reflective thinking. The sense which it is to make in theological terms cannot be understood from the standpoint of "subjective intelligence," or reflection, where the self as "I" occupies the chief position. Initially a problem is presented by the conflict between the sense of "I" (the thought "I") and the sense of "God" (the thought "God"). The thought contained in the word "I" is the source of all categories and the final subject of all judgments. "I" am always a subject and never a predicate in a judgment as well as the subject of last resort in every judgment; grammatically, "I" am always a substantive and never an adjective. Every judgment is traceable to one who makes the judgment, and the word "I" designates that one in its final recourse. Even when a judgment is about something else, as it is in "This is a tree," the actual judging that is embodied in the words is the doing of some one, an "I" making the judgment. At a step removed we may say that "he" or the other person makes the judgment, but still it is "I" who judge that the other is the source of a particular judgment. In this way, what is meant by "I," as I say and think it, is the original subject to which judgments can be traced.

This capital position of the self puts "egoistic" reflection at odds with the thinking required to understand the sense of "God is the word and the word is God." For the sense of this proposition is to demand that "I" give up my capital position as the one making the judgments. Yet how is that possible? Obviously, it is not possible when thinking is the activity of the subject, or self, and being is that toward which thinking is directed. Some other mode of thinking is needed. Like the word "I," "God" designates one who can never be the predicate in a judgment and whose name, grammatically, can never be an adjective. God can never be predicated of another, and of God the only predication to be made is that God is God: *God* is God, and God is *God*. "God" is unconditionally what "I" am conditionally. To say something or someone is "God," if by that we understand a predication on the order of "This is a tree," is to contradict the sense of "God" as much as saying that something is "I" contradicts the sense of "I."

Consequently, assertions on the order of "God is the word and the word is God" can be regarded as true by "subjective intelligence" only if the two terms are regarded as two different names designating the same sense and referent. "God is the word" has the same character, then, as "God is Yahweh"—the one who is called "God" in English is called "Yahweh" in Hebrew. This is the only possible way in which the assertion as formulated can be true for reflective thought. Otherwise, "The word is God" would have to be interpreted as ascribing deity to the word, that is, as using the predicate term "God" to modify the word; "God is the word" would ascribe something other than deity to God. But the reflective interpretation runs counter to the intention of the theological assertion of identity between God and word. If that intention is to be true, some form of thinking other than reflective judgment is required.

Daub's contention is that reflective thinking can be transcended, and the propositon "God is the word and the word is God" mediates the transition. Indeed, on his reading, the arguments for the existence of God—the *Reflexionsbeweise*—serve to show the incapacity of reflective thinking to deal with the matter of God's being. Anselm's argument may come closest to being a genuine theological proof, but it still has the form of a reflective proof, and for that reason it shows most clearly the self-restriction that reflective thought encounters. The theological content of the identity between God and the word cannot be uncovered until reflection gives way to another kind of thinking.

How it can do so Daub explains by reference to the act of abstraction. In objective knowledge we abstract from the subject in order to show the object in itself; in knowledge of the subject, we abstract from objectivity and let the subject show itself in its expressions. Both of these abstractions occur within reflective thinking. But a third abstraction is also possible; when it is performed, thinking is transmuted. In this step we abstract from subjects and objects altogether in the interest of a realm in which the division between subjects and objects no longer applies. To do so only requires an act of the will. The abstraction is facilitated, however, by the demand upon reflection made by the thought of God, which is one of the many reflective thoughts, and by an "interest" simply in the name, the word, and the thought expressed by "God" itself. The reflective proofs of God oblige reflection to see that it cannot adjudicate the question of the reality of God at all. Having seen that, reflection need not blindly revert to unthinking faith. It can remain interested in the word "God" itself without regard to whether there is an object which corresponds to it. This interest in the word and idea "God" prevents doubt about the existence of God from becoming sheer despair in the matter, and it is the means through which reflection is shaped as "speculation."

The thinking which is guided by nothing other than an interest in the word and what the word might disclose directs attention to the words as they name something, convey a meaning, and signify a referent. We reflect, as Daub puts it, on the name in relation to itself rather than in its relation to any object or subject that we might otherwise know; we reflect on the thought (or meaning) in relation to itself instead of to us; and on the object of the thought in relation to that object itself instead of to us. The key phrase is "in relation to itself." In the course of the essay, it becomes clear that reflecting on the name, the thought, and the object "in relation to itself" amounts to working out the inner connections of the various elements in the word. The "name" seen "in relation to itself" is the vocable, the linguistic *sign*, in relation to its *sense* and its *referent*; the "thought" seen "in relation to itself" is the sense in relation to the sign which carries it and to the object which it signifies; and the "object" that is "in relation to itself" is the referent in relation to the sense of the word which signifies it and to the vocable that carries that sense. In short, "egoistic" reflection that transcends itself becomes a reflection on language. It has to do not with the relations between thinking and being, subjectivity and objectivity, but with the relations among the sign (the "name"), the sense (the "thought"), and the significance and referent (the "object") as these elements are brought together in language. Accordingly, instead of asking what God is in relation to our thinking or in relation to the objects in the world, one asks what relation the elements of naming, meaning, and signifying have to one another in the word "God" itself. These questions cannot be answered by attending to something other than the word; they must be answered by reflecting on language to see how it holds the name, the thought, and the object together, and how each leads to the other.

This "speculative" reflection, directed toward language as the realm in which being and thinking are together and in which therefore the division between subject and object does not obtain, yields results different from those of the reflection in which "I" am thinking about the being of "it" and in so doing retain a capital position for the self. If *I* try to distinguish the thought of God from subjects and objects—that is to say, if reflection seeks to show that the meaning in "God" does not signify any subject or object—the result is that I can say such things as "God is word-like" but not "God is the word and the word is God." For in the second of these propositions God is made a predicate of another subject, and just this contradicts the meaning of God as unconditional subject. The religion that corresponds to this kind of thinking is the religion of the "mononymous subject." Its basic thought is that nothing is God, only God is God; it is founded on the position that God cannot be identical with the word and the word cannot be God, for that would deny the deity of God as the unconditional subject. God cannot *be* anything, and nothing can *be* God; God can only *be like* this or that, and in turn they can only *be like* God.

On the other hand, if, in a transition to another kind of thinking which is both subjective and objective at once, I as a subject acknowledge the power of the meaning of the word over reflection (so that my thinking is guided by the meaning conveyed through reflecting on the word "God" itself), then the fact that *I* make a distinction between God and every subject or object is of no consequence; for I see that the distinction between God and everything lies in the meaning of the word itself. My thinking that God is not the word and the word is not God is at the same time the thinking on the part of the word "God." The power that enables us to think that God is not identical with any person or thing resides in the word "God" itself, the word that permits us to become, as Daub puts it, "participant in" the thought of God. The *word* "God" is the unconditional subject, in which particular thinkers participate when they do their own thinking. The thought "God" is designated in each language by that word which speakers of the language use to name the identity between thought and reality that is the origin or principle of language. In each language there is a word which designates the unity of meaning and reality, a word which names that unity, means that unity, and is that unity. As a result, the thought of God is a thought that, though it can be borne by many different sounds in the various languages, is mononymous without being fixed. The one God with the one name can call himself "God" in one language, "Dieu" in another and "Allah" in still another. But these are all the same name, and it is the same one who names himself in them. The religion that can at least acknowledge this mononymous thought, which is the condition for knowing the truth in religion, is monotheistic without excluding polytheism.

There is another way of stating what Daub sets forth. As far as reflective thinking is concerned, "God" is unconditionally the subject only in a negative manner. What "God" means is "not-I" and "not-this." To say, for example, that *God* is omnipotent is to assert that, at any event, it is not I who am omnipotent and not anything else that is omnipotent. God is the subject who appears as the negation of any other subject and of any object. This is as far as reflection can go. "God" appears on its horizon only as the unmasterable negation. God is *God*—and not anything or anyone else; *God* is God—no one and nothing else than God is God. This is, incidentally, not the same as saying "There is no God"; for, strictly speaking, what is being asserted is that there is a God, but this God "exists" only as the negation of all concrete subjects and objects. He appears as the not-I along with the subject "I" and as the not-this along with the objective thing: I am I, not-I is God; this is a tree, not-this is God. This is a more exact way of stating that the being of God eludes adjudication by reflection—God appears in reflection and to reflection, and thus would seem to be someone or something; but he appears only as the negative of subjects and objects and therefore seems to be no one and nothing. The thought of God thus defeats reflection.

So defeated—and it is a *self*-defeat, as much reflection's own doing as something that befalls it—reflection has the opportunity to become "speculation." It remains interested in the word "God," which can do this. For further progress it needs only to give up its concern to identify whether God names a subject or an object or nothing, in favor of following the word in its own movement. In this progress the agent of the thought is at one and the same time the personal subject and the word. To illustrate the way in which the two agents can be together one might think of the music made by playing a violin. On the one hand, the person who draws the bow across the strings and fingers the notes is the one who makes the music; but on the other hand, it is the violin itself that is sounding. Members of the audience hear a sound whose agent is twofold; both assertions are correct: The violin is playing, the violinist is playing, the music. Thinking of thinking by reflecting on words is similar. When a thought is formed through words, both assertions are correct: We form the thought, and the word forms the thought. We think; the word thinks. When we think the meaning that is carried by words, there are simultaneously two agents of the thought—the word and our intellectual effort. Both assertions are correct: The word means something, we mean something, when meaning is conveyed by language. The meaning of a word is both the meaning associated with the acoustic or visual sign (the sense the word carries) and the meaning we think when we hear or read the word.

Initially the word "God," as Daub follows it, discloses a threefold determination: 1) it names the thinking being that is "independent of subjectivity and objectivity," a thinking being that is not-I; 2) it names my thought of that thinking being; and 3) it names my thought of the word "God," which expresses that thinking being. That is to say, the name can designate the object of the thought (identified as the independent thinking being), or someone's thought of that object, or the thought as communicated or put into language (the common, communicable thought). "God" names an intended object; it names also my act of thinking when I understand the word; and it names the communicability of the object. (Similarly, "tree" is the name of a physical object, it is also the name of what I am thinking when I understand the word, and finally it is how that physical object is commonly understood. It designates a thing, a meaning, and a word.) Reflection on each of these three different elements, or determinations, entails a different kind of abstraction. In the first case, we abstract from the self and refer the name to what it is a thought of—we use the name "tree" in order to think of the physical object. In the second case we abstract from the referent and refer the name to our thought of the referent—we use the word "tree" to designate what we have in mind. In the third case we abstract from the self and the distinctions it makes between subject and object and refer the name to the communicated form of that object—we use the word "tree" itself as the object. In this last case the word refers to itself. It is abstracted from the distinction between subject and object since it is at one and the same time a thought of the thing and the thing in a thought. The communicated form of an object is that object put into a word.

These three abstractions can be applied to the word "God." If we use the word in order to think of an object (the first abstraction), none appears, except perhaps a postulated metaphysical object. If it is to designate our thought of the unconditional subject, a contradiction emerges between the notion of an unconditional subject and the fact that it is intended as the object of our thinking. Hence, the thought of God is a nihility as much as the existence of God. But if we use the word "God" as the communicated form of the unconditional subject, then the word is at one and the same time our thought of the unconditional subject and the unconditional subject in our thought.

This may be explained (not in Daub's manner) by reference to the way in which the word "God" is the negation of the absence of any object (in the first abstraction) and any subject (in the second abstraction). As an objective reality, God may be nothing, but the *word* "God" is the negation of that nothing. Unlike the word "nothing," which in being not nothing is self-negating, the word "God" negates nothing by being something. If nothing is, then the word "nothing" must vanish, but the word "God" stays around. As the word "God," God is both nothing (no object and no subject) and the negation of nothing (a word). Similarly, God who is a self-contradictory idea, when considered as a thought, is the negation of that negation when it is a word. With respect to both of these abstractions the word "God" negates the negative—the way in which the negation of nothing appears as a reality is as the word "God," and the way in which the negation of the ego is enacted in thought is through the word "God."

A fourth determination is added to these three (the name of a being, the name of a meaning, the name of a word) when the name is connected to the thought and simultaneously to the object of the thought, as it is in the sentence "God is the word (or: the word is God)." With the name "God" is associated another name "word," which designates what is the object for the thought "God." What we think when we understand the word "God" is the same as what we ascertain, or apprehend, when we are presented with a word. (The word "tree" refers to a physical object; the word "God" refers to a word, or the word.) "Intelligence [subjective reflection] cannot believe that the name 'word' is not only [a word], but something quite other [than a word]—that it is the actual object of the thought designated with the name 'God' . . ." ("Logos," p. 398). To believe and know this, Daub continues, reflection must let itself be "determined through the thought" in abstraction from its relation to the subject; it must reflect only on the relation of the thought (the sense of the word "God") to its object (the givenness of the word). In doing so, reflection (as it reflects on the relation between what is meant by the word "God" and what is given by the word "word") comes to know that it is the word through which the sense has been communicated (it is through the word "God" that the meaning or the thought of God is commonly understood) and that it is through a sign (a name), which is the same as the sense, that reflection takes part in the content of the thought (the significance of the sense). Acknowledging this is made possible for intelligence on the basis of the thought (the meaning) "God": the content of "God" is not I; it is, rather, the content of the object of the thought, or the referent. "God *was* the word, and because he was that, the world could *begin* to be, man to live and think, and the thought which it (the word) contains and which in itself is identical with the name could *become* man's in the name 'God' and the like" (p. 399, emphasis in text).

Unlike a categorical judgment, in which "God was the word" would mean that "God" is the subject-term and "word" the predicate and in which the meaning of "word" and the meaning of "God" are the same, the sense of "God is the word" is that the meaning carried by "word" has as its content, or significance, the meaning carried by "God." The meaning of "God" signifies the meaning of "word." This relation is based on the fact that "word" is an "object to itself"; that is to say, a word is what it names, the word "word" is a word. This is not the relation of subject to predicate, but of a meaning to its instantiation. The meaning of "word" is (let us formulate it so): a thought-thing that is a signifier; and this meaning is instantiated by the word "God." The connection, then, which is formulated as the identity of God and word is that a word is instantiated as word only when someone *thinks* it, and God (the unconditional subject) is instantiated only when someone *says* or *writes* the word "God"; and the word "word" is instantiated by itself—the figure w–o–r–d becomes what it names when it is thought and said (or written).

This is the point in Daub's essay at which a reflexive dimension is attained. "God" is a word, and it also designates the word. This last determination precludes referring the connection between the meaning of God and the word "God" to our own reflective thought. To say that what the word "God" signifies is not an object or a subject or nothing, but the word, is to assert what is implicit in the meaning of the word "God" itself. Thus, a reflection on the word "God" brings out that the sign and meaning and referent are joined with one another in the word "God" itself. A word is an object—something perceptibly there; but we can perceive it as a word, instead of as a meaningless sound or sight, only by an understanding added to physical perception. Thus, what distinguishes the written French word *son* from the written English word *son* lies not in their appearance, but in our understanding of their meaning. God is the unity of thinking and being, but this is perceptible only in the word that names it. To think of God is to think of the thought that is independent of us and others; to think of language is to think of the being that is independent of physical objects.

The formulation that God is the word and that the word is God thus means that the thought which negates subjectivity (God is not the same as I) has as its referent the object which negates objectivity (a word is not a thing but a meaning in a thing). God means a subject who is never identical with the subject that "I" am; in that sense, his unconditional subjectivity negates subjectivity. A word is an object that is never identical with what its acoustic or visual figure is; in that sense, it negates objectivity. For a word to appear as a word, and not a mute thing, it is required that I think its content; and for God to *be* something that can be called a thinking, it is required that he appear in a sign that carries the thought (a word, the word "God"). This relation of word to God is made in what is in effect a reflexive judgment. It formulates the notion that when the thinking process as such, which is always a thinking of being and which is named by the word "God," is transformed from pure activity into an object, the result is the object that the word "word" refers to: language. Conversely, when language is translated into the pure activity which it embodies, the result is the thinking process as such, which "God" names. A reflection on language leads to the thinking of being, and the communication of the thinking of being leads to the word "God." "God" names the one whose being is thinking—he is not a person or a thing; "word" names an object whose being is thinking—he is not a person or a thing; "word" names an object whose thinking is being—a meaningless sound "is" not a word; and "God is the word and the word is God" asserts that what we think in the word "God" and what we perceive in the word "word" are the same in the different. But this is a judgment from the standpoint of reflexivity. The meaning of assertions about God corresponds to the reality in the givenness of language. That is their truth. But this is a truth about truth insofar as the meaning of the word "God" is the same as its reality (hence an embodiment of the true) and insofar as the reality of the word "word" is the same as its meaning (hence embodying the true). The word "God" instantiates what it signifies, and the word "word" means what it instantiates.

The instantiating feature is of decisive importance, for it places "God" and "word" among such other demonstrative names as "I," "this," "here," and "now," which display what they designate as soon as they are named. The person who thinks or says "I" thereby becomes the referent that the word signifies. The word "this" (as in "This is a tree") itself points out the object to which it refers; that of which we say "this" becomes the object meant. The word "God" belongs in this list insofar as it actually instantiates the negative. To say "God" is to become the sign pointing away from itself. To the extent that the word "God" has instantiating power, its referent is provided by the very thought or speaking of the word. "God" instantiates the negation of the subject, as "I" posits it, and the negation of an object, as "this" shows it. It therefore drives a subject first out of itself to some object—"God" as "not-I" opens my eyes to what is other than I, and what I see first is some object, a "this." But "God" also instantiates a "not-this," and hence it urges me to look still further. It instantiates a continual opening, related to whatever comes into view, but never filled out by anything. "God" thus actually instantiates the dynamic openness of being in the world. Aquinas said that the movement from potentiality to actuality provided the connectedness among all things in the world. Seeing movement, the mind is driven from one thing to the next in the direction of the infinite. But then the word "God" is inserted, and this makes it unnecessary to proceed to infinity. The word "God" thus instantiates the negation of the infinitude of the *procedere*. To say, in this setting, that God is the first cause (what everyone calls God is what we reflectively think of as the first cause) is to draw a connection between what is instantiated by the word "God" and what is understood as the result of a reflection on the movement of the world.

The same can be applied to Daub's remarks. "God is the word" may have the sense that the negative which "God" instantiates is connected with what is understood as a reflection on language. What is instantiated when we say or think "God" is signification, so that to say "God" is to turn what is said as "I" into a signifier of another. In this sense Daub can speak of the *Resignation* of the self: the self "re-signs" itself, it turns itself from an autonomous self-referring subject into a subject that signifies another. What is instantiated by "God" is the same as what is understood as the result of a reflection on language—that language is a unity of thinking and being such that its character is to be a signifier of otherness. A word is a sign, a thought-thing, an object carrying a meaning and a meaning as an object.

What is true of the instantiating capacity of the single word "God" holds then also for the proposition "God[=not-I] is God [=not-this]." This proposition can be inscribed upon any proposition to turn its meaning into a sign of another meaning and its reality into the sign of another reality. If the true and the false are the reflective objects to which whole propositions refer, as Frege stated (p. 63), then what the proposition "God is God" instantiates is a negation of reflection in its seeing of the true or the false. The true and the false and the reflective act become signs of something else.

If we relate Daub's discussion to the *Deus est* in Aquinas's five ways and to Barth's interpretation of Anselm, then his essay calls attention to the place where the theological matter is at issue: not the name "first cause" to designate that in the world which precludes a *procedere in infinitum*, and not some other name, such as *id quo majus cogitari nequit*, but the linguistic act in which the name "God" is connected with another name, and the nature of the "is" in saying the one is the other. The very matter which remains in the background in Aquinas and in Barth now comes into the foreground. Barth declared the identity between "God" and "that than which no greater can be thought" to be the presupposition of faith which is the basis of the proof; and Aquinas simply noted that everyone makes the connection between the two names "first cause" and "God." In Daub's interpretation of the identity between God and word it is just this connection between two names that is the *object* of reflection, not its presupposition or an addendum to it. Anselm's proof (in Barth's reworking) may show how the phrase "that than which no greater can be thought" is a word-unit whose very meaning (the thought of what cannot be merely a thought) prevents thought from being enclosed in itself. But it does not show how this word-unit is to be connected with the word "God." It presupposes the very matter that becomes the object of Daub's theological reflection. When we do reflect on the *proposition* "God is the word," then we see the identity of God with himself. "The name [viz., the word "God"] is identical with the thought" asserts that in the word "God" the sign is the same as the meaning: the meaning of "God" is that it is a sign, and its function is to signify and to turn everything into a signifier without pointing out what is signified.

Applied, for example, to what Augustine discovers in his interrogation of creation, this is to say that the name "God," as the not-I of every subject and the not-this of every object, brings out the signifying capacity of the whole creation: "I interrogated the mass of the world about my God, and it responded to me: not I am [he], but he made me" (*Conf.*, 10:6,9). All things say of God only "Non sumus," "We are not." When Augustine then presses them further: "Tell me then of my God, . . . tell me something about him," they all exclaim with a loud voice, "Ipse fecit nos," "He made us." "My interrogation was my intention, and their response was their shining visage" (*Conf.*, 10:6,9). The intention was expressed in a query about *Deus meus*; the sight of everything was interpreted with reference to the intention of "God." Everything appeared as pointing away from itself—"non sumus"—and as being able to point out what it pointed to only in the words "He made us." In that sense everything is a sign carrying a meaning, everything is a "word."

If the meaning of "God" is that it is a sign whose function is to signify without displaying what is signified, except as the power to transmute things into signs, then it is correlative with the word "word." "Word" too is the sign of a sign. But it displays what it signifies by being what it names. The word "God" accordingly always points to a referent, by the "not-this-but-another" that it inscribes upon subjects and objects, but no person or thing can fill in the expectation of that referent. The word "word" does fill in the referent. In both of the figures "word" and "God," the sense is "an acoustic or visual figure of pointing to . . ."; they both are signs of a sign, or names of a name. But "word" also *is* what it signifies. Hence, the literal referent of the word "God" is, finally, the word "word"—the phenomenon of language, and the word-character that the name "God" instantiates in everything.

The connection between "God" and "word" is made through a reflection on the word itself. The sign and sense are identical (since the sense of "God" is to be a sign), and the sense and object are identical (since what is signified by the word "God" is the word "God"). The identity between sense and object (referent), however, is mediated by the word "word," as the sign of a sign. The meaning of the word "God" corresponds to the reality of the word "word." This semantic reflection differs from other reflection because it is directed to the being of thinking as present in language. In object-related, mundane thought, one thinks of the being of the thing, the unity of a physical percept and a notion, which appears at one time as meaning and at another time as reality. But a reflection on the relation between "God" and "word" as given in the words themselves is a thinking of being that at one and the same time is meaning and reality.

One can think of a word as the being of thinking (the

embodiment of the act of thinking, or the thought as an object of thinking), and also as the thinking in being (a thought of the object, or the object as a thought). A word is a thought when the thought is other than itself, and it is a thing when the thing is other than itself. In this way a word is an identity in difference, the embodiment of otherness.

But Daub's exposition of this kind of thinking does not yet distinguish between that part of it which is hermeneutical and that part of it which is verificational. In the one respect, "God is the word and the word is God" asserts that what is naively understood in the word "God" is the same as what is explicated in the concept of the word. It is neither an empty tautology ("God is God"), nor a citation of two names for one thing (" 'God' and 'word' are two names for a thinking that is being"), nor a judgment in which wordiness is attributed to God ("God is wordlike, spiritual"). It is, rather, an assertion of the "being" that appears in language as a synthesis of naive understanding and reflective concept. Through the word "God" we understand, and through the word "word" we state what it is we understand. The same thing happens when the naive understanding of the words "This is a tree" is put into reflective terms which state what it is that has been understood, namely, being as it appears in the unity of our perception and our notion of a physical object.

In another respect, however, "God is word" asserts that the word "God" and the proposition "God is God" are capable of being inscribed upon things so as to "re-sign" them, or turn them into symbols of the essence of God. For this aspect of the matter a hermeneutical reflection is insufficient; some reference to the reality that is given independently is required. Here the limitations of an abstraction from subjects and objects come into view. For, although reflection on language does make clear the independence of hermeneutical reflection (the mediation between naive understanding and reflective thought) from natural and ethical thinking, it does not overcome the split in reflection itself. This can be seen if attention is called to how the experience of truth appears in the hermeneutical reflection, that is, in the reflection which is borne by language in the movement from naive to critical understanding. Truth appears here by virtue of a *third* language in which can be said both what thinking is and what being thinks. That the meaning of the word "God" and the referent of the word "word" correspond to each other, in the sense that the naive understanding of the word "God" is recovered in the reflective grasp of language, is said in a discourse different from both the discourse about language (in which we say what language is) and the discourse about God (in which we say what God means). What God means is "sign of, pointer to"; what language is is "sign of, pointer to." What God means and what language is are the same; to say what the word "God" means (namely, the unconditional subject) is the same as to say what language, or the word, is (unconditional subject). But the notion of sign and pointing are in a metalanguage with respect both to theological language naively understood and to logological language reflectively grasped. God *means* a certain negation (not-I, not-this); a word, or language as such, *is* a certain negation (not the thingness of a thing, but the thought-thing); God means otherness, words are otherness; God signifies the otherness of subject and object; words are the otherness of subject and object. But these assertions are a part neither of the discourse about the meaning of God nor of the discourse about the being of language. Hence, reflection in the medium of language, as a thinking which is both subjective and objective at once, gives way to its own reflexivity and occasions a split in reflexivity that is a repetition of the split in reflection. For the identity between the meaning of God and the being of language (and conversely) is one that reflexivity here (in some persons) sees and reflexivity there (in others) does not see. In effect the assertion at issue here is "God is God as the word, and the word is word as God." The sense is that in the word "God" as well as in the whole of language one sees the way in which God is God. God is God *as* word.[2] Similarly, the converse statement about language is not what language is (it "is" not God), but how the essence of language is shown—language is language as the word "God," i.e., as the word whose meaning is its reality and whose reality is its meaning, and which therefore shows the essence of language as thought-thing or thinking-being.

Reflexivity and the Symbol of the Cross

To say "God" on the part of a self as "I" is to turn the "I" of the self into a sign of another by a self-negation that is a "re-signation," a "re-signing" of the subject. "God" instantiates that transformation. This thought provides a transition to the way in which the truth of truth emerges. The truth of truth is not found in language alone but in a reflexive dimension in reality which corresponds to the reflexivity of the self and which is grasped by the very division between reflection here and reflection there. This can be elucidated by reference to what Tillich calls the symbol of the cross, which in the context of Christian theology signifies that Jesus "sacrifices himself as Jesus to himself as the Christ" and therein is the mediator of God.

In a discussion of the criteria of the truth of faith, Tillich states the criterion in two ways. Subjectively "faith is true if it adequately expresses an ultimate concern," and "adequacy" means "the power of expressing an ultimate concern in such a way that it creates reply, action, communication" (*DF*, p. 96). This is the criterion by which to determine whether a symbol is still a living symbol, that is, whether it manifests anything at all. The objective criterion is that "faith is true if its content is really ultimate" (p. 96). In summary form, the criterion "of the truth of faith . . . is that it implies an element of self-negation" (p. 97). The most adequate symbol is the one "which expresses not only the ultimate but also its own lack of ultimacy" (p. 97). Tillich continues: "Christianity expresses itself in such a symbol in contrast to all other religions, namely, in the Cross of the Christ. Jesus could not have been the Christ without sacrificing himself as Jesus to himself as the Christ" (pp. 97-98). Tillich refers to this as an "infallible truth" of faith, and the only such. "The only infallible truth of faith, the one in which the ultimate itself is unconditionally manifest, is that any truth of faith stands under a yes-or-no [yes-and-no] judgment" (p. 98). With reference to the symbol of the cross, which is identical with "the Protestant principle," he says "the criterion contains a Yes—it does not reject any truth of faith in whatever form it may appear in the history of faith—and it contains a No—it does not accept any truth of faith as ultimate except the one that no man possesses it" (p. 98).

The reflexive character of the symbol is indicated in the way it is formulated: the "infallible truth" is the truth that no one possesses the truth, and this is not imposed on faith but is in the symbol of faith. The self-relativization contained in this particular experience of truth has the character both of an experience of truth and of an experience which puts truth in relation to its opposite. The truth about truth is experienced as the possibility of its being other than how it is actually experienced. There is no experience of truth that is itself an experience of *the* one and only truth, except in the reflexive form of the experience of the relativity of truth.

Experience of the truth in the symbol of the cross is thus different from other experiences of truth in symbols by virtue of its reflexivity or self-relativization. What the symbol of the cross symbolizes is the symbolic character of all symbols. If the distinguishing mark of a religious symbol is that it elicits and expresses the ultimate in the form of concern, then every religious symbol is an ultimate concern. Every such symbol, however, has a limited range; it depends upon cultural and historical conditions. This is ascertainable simply through reflection and ordinary observation. Symbols elicit and express concern for some persons, but not for others. Some symbols which once were effective are no longer effective. Symbols are involved with the split in reflection itself. That a given symbol is real for M but not for N does not entail that M is unreflective and N reflective. It may mean only that the symbol which speaks to M does not speak to N; for M it is a reality, ascertainable as such, for N it is a mere possibility.

The question is whether this relativity of symbols is introduced only by reflection or whether there is another symbol, of a second order, which symbolizes it. Tillich's account of the symbol of the cross is important because it treats the cross as a second-order symbol, which symbolizes this relativity of all symbols; it bears a relation to other symbols that is to the object of experience what the reflexive self is to the first-order subject. When identity in difference (what is seen as truth) not only is what we can see reflectively but also expresses and elicits concern, then (in Tillich's terms) it is a symbol as well as an object. But the symbol of the cross is to other symbols of truth what reflexivity is to reflection. Reflexivity can see that reflection is capable of seeing both the true and the false (it can see the duality of reflection); the symbol of the cross symbolizes the depth that comprises both the true and the false.

The experience of truth in the symbol of the cross is "infallible" just because it can comprise both the true and the false as they appear to reflection. Abstractly formulated, this symbol symbolizes that all symbols are of relative validity; its absoluteness does not exclude, but includes, its relativity. What the symbol of the cross symbolizes in Christianity is this: At any given time, it is possible for a person to determine whether the figure of Jesus as presented in the New Testament is a symbol of the ultimate, a symbol of the essence of God, or, in Tillich's phrasing, an ultimate concern. It is possible therefore to experience the assertion "Jesus is the ultimate concern" as true or as false. The assertion is verifiable. Let us suppose that in a given case it turns out to be true because the figure of Jesus does indeed elicit a response of ultimate concern, does make action possible, and does enable the person to communicate the reality of that concern. If the true is experienced in the figure of Jesus without reference to the symbol of the cross, then it may later turn out to be false under the same test as the one under which now it shows the true. The figure of Jesus may at some time in the future no longer elicit and express the ultimate in the form of concern. When tested for its truth, the assertion "Jesus is the ultimate concern" will then be false. If, however, the experience of the true in the figure of Jesus is connected with the symbol of the cross, then this negative possibility is anticipated in the experience of the truth. Since what the cross symbolizes is the relativity of all symbolic expressions, the failure of the figure of Jesus to elicit and express ultimate concern will still be in accord with what the symbol expresses. It confirms the relativity of the material that makes up symbols. Even further, if the symbol of the cross itself should no longer effectively symbolize the relativity of all symbols, this possibility too is anticipated in the experience of truth in the symbol of the cross. In short, if *at any time* the symbol of the cross has been experienced as true, then this truth anticipates and allows all other experiences of the true and the false. The depth of truth is experienced by way of the true, but it is capable of including its opposite within itself.

The importance of the symbol of the cross for the split in reflection is that it contains an experience of truth that warrants the appearance of both the true and the false to reflection. This experience is itself reflexive, rather than reflective. The symbol of the cross is the reflexive dimension of other symbols; it is the reality which corresponds to the meaning of the proposition " ' "This . . ." is true' is true."

In contrast to what Daub sets out as the thinking in which reflection is transcended by a movement of language, this description maintains the distinction between reality and meaning. The conception that Daub sets forth of a thinking that is not a thinking by a subject of an object, but a thinking that is both subjective and objective at once, runs the risk of losing reality, as does Kierkegaard's knight of infinite resignation, instead of gaining it, as does the knight of faith. That is to say, it courts the danger of so losing interest in extralinguistic reality that the experience of truth is no longer possible. It eliminates the difference in the identity, by seeing language as simultaneously the meaning and the reality. Reflexive thinking is, by contrast, still a thinking on the part of an "I"; it is "I" who think about the experience of truth (which itself is a thinking about the relation between meaning and reality). And the symbol of the cross is a reality in the reality of the figure of Jesus, given independently of the meaning. The self in this relation is reflexive and not only reflective or world-related, and the other is a reflexive truth and not only truth or a world-object; but it is still a relation between the self and the other, and the truth of truth is given upon a real object in relation to a meaning. In idealist speculation the reality that is given up is not gotten back; it is given up in favor of an indifference to the relation between meaning and reality and a contentment with meaning regardless of reality.

Truth in the symbol of the cross needs to be seen only once in order for it to play this rôle; but it must be seen at least once, otherwise one cannot decide whether reflection is ultimately incompetent to determine the true and the false. To see that a division in reflection does not destroy the experience of truth, but deepens it by disclosing another dimension is what decides the matter. From the standpoint of this experience, reflection and religion, the one denying and the other affirming the appearing God, can be related to each other as a later and an earlier stage of consciousness, both having to do with truth; the existence of something as divine is remembered in reflection as part of its own past, the naive is remembered in the critical, and both are elements in the truth. Prereflective religion accepts the appearing God as God; reflection rejects the appearance. From the standpoint of the reflexive experience of the symbol of the cross, the reality intended, but not yet distinguished, by religion is a reality that makes its appearance in the movement between religion and reflection. The untruth of all existent gods, which is exposed by reflection, is the essence of the God who is God. Truth for religion consisted in the relation in which consciousness neither could nor wished to withdraw itself from the impression of the appearing God; for reflection the untruth of religion consists in the ascertainment that no object can be godly. From the standpoint of the reflexive experience of the truth of truth in the symbol of the cross, what religion receives and what reflection dispells (by its critical questioning) are two phases of the God who is the depth of truth. Again, the ambiguity of the assertion "God is" today is seen reflexively as an anticipation of the symbol of the cross. Finally, that "God is God as the man Jesus" divides reflection within itself is seen to be the self-relativization of the symbol. Hence, the reflexive experience of the truth of truth comprises the relative experience of the true and the relative experience of the untrue or the false.

There is no reason why theology must assert as true something whose truth cannot be experienced. This is not to say that some restricted criterion of truth must be employed. But it is to say that what is asserted to be true is capable of being understood and that this meaning is capable of being compared with the reality to which it refers. That some assertions which one would like to see true turn out to be otherwise is a hazard that theology shares with other discourse. The risk neither can nor should be evaded by taking refuge in unchallengeable assertions of faith. Indeed, the experience of the truth of the symbol of the cross makes just the opposite so, inasmuch as the true and the false are incorporated into the depth of truth that this symbol expresses. If the depth of the true and the false can also be experienced through the false, this does not alter the result. Indeed, there are reasons to think that Nirvana expresses the depth of reality by way of the negative whereas the kingdom of heaven does so by way of the positive, in each case with the depth including both. What is important for the experience of truth is only that this depth can *at least* be experienced by way of the true in a symbol whose truth, once seen, permits both the experience of the true and of the false.

When Augustine discerned, as an answer to his interrogation, the reply "Not we are God, but God made us," he went on to ask, "Why does the world not say the same to everyone?" He answered his own question by saying that it is not that the *moles mundi* changes its voice, but that "to that one it is silent, to this one it speaks" (*Conf.*, 10:6, 10). Then he corrects himself by adding, "Nay, rather, it speaks to all, but those understand who compare the voice they heard without with the truth within. . . . For it is truth that says to me: Your God is not the heaven and earth nor any body."

The first part of Augustine's explanation is right—for some the "mass of the earth" is a sign; it "speaks" to them of another. For others it is only what it literally is, an appearing object, which signifies nothing more. Whether it is the one or the other depends upon whether it speaks (as a word) or does not speak (as a thing). It has the freedom to do both. But, contrary to Augustine, from the standpoint of the experience of the symbol of the cross, both experiences are included in the truth. The mass of the world does not literally speak, but it may be made to speak when "God is God," inscribed upon it, turns it from a mute object into a "word." Whether it does thus speak depends only in part upon whether the theological language is explicitly inscribed upon it; for in part it also depends upon the freedom of this language to disclose or not to disclose at given times.

Theology has the task of inscribing "God" upon all names, "God is" upon all events, and "God is God" upon all identities. In carrying out that task it has the intention of speaking the truth so that the truth can be seen or heard. Sometimes it will, and sometimes it will not, succeed in this effort. It is free to acknowledge its failures as well as its successes, and to let its assertions be open to experiential testing. On occasion it must risk using language other than "God," and discourse about God, in order to say what it has to say, but even so its responsibility is for theological language. For the sake of truth, theology has to answer for the word "God," the tale "God is," and the judgment "God is God." But it does not have to answer for God, the be-ing of God, and the identity of God, which answer for themselves when they answer.

Notes

Chapter 1

1.) The difference between Bonaventure and Aquinas is not in the use of the necessity of thought to replace direct perception of objects but in whether that necessity amounts to an intuition of its object or whether, on the contrary, it only leads up to the point where the mind is free to assent to an object as a matter of faith. The Thomistic position is given an interpretation in Karl Rahner's *Spirit in World.*

2.) Empirical thought can be constrained against its own rules, as a simple example shows. By the rule of identity, if a thing is white it cannot be nonwhite (if A is A, it cannot be not-A). Yet every actual object that fits under the class at all is both white and nonwhite, no object is purely an example of a white thing, and we must, accordingly, think of any such object as white in some respects and not white in others. Hence the abstract formula for the relation between pure thought and empirical reality, the formula expressing the openness of thinking to being, is always the very formula indicating the impossibility of thought—that of contradiction. "Being" designates what, strictly, cannot be thought but is always presenting itself to be thought. Our actual knowledge of the world is thus a compromise between the necessity of thinking in itself and the impossibility of thinking which is the necessity of being, the necessity imposed by entities. Fichte's *Wissenschaftslehre* showed that this contradiction lies in thinking itself—the original formula for the activity of thinking is not identity or contradiction but identity in contradiction, or limitation; science, or self-conscious knowledge, is composed of statements not with the form "A is A" but with the form "A is A limited by not-A," an original synthesis a priori. Fichte, therefore, rejected as spurious Kant's question of how synthetic judgments a priori are possible because it assumes that such judgments need an explanation in a way that analytical a priori and synthetic a posteriori ones do not.

184

3.) White concludes that the correspondence theory is basically correct; what is meant when an assertion is true is "that what is said has said things as they actually are; it has stated a fact" (p. 128).

4.) Paradigms are sentences in which there is a one-to-one correlation of the words of the paradigm with the elements of that of which it is a paradigm. The words "He told me he would do it, and he did" express an experience of truth, but they do not compose a paradigm of it. "What he told me turned out to be true" comes closer. " 'This is a tree' is true" is paradigmatic because each of its elements is correlated with an element of reflective experience.

5.) " 'This is a tree' is a sequence of four words" is not a judgment about a mental act, of course, since it treats the words as physical things. It is on a par with "This is a tree" except that what it refers to is not a natural object but a set of vocables. If the question is raised whether " 'This is a tree' is a sequence of four words" is true, one counts the words to ascertain whether there are four of them (if the article "a" is counted as a separate word). If it is asked whether " 'This is a tree' is a judgment" is true, one must reflect on the act that takes place in thinking the words through. Whether a sentence is a judgment is determined not by the words in it, but by the mental process of which it is the product and of which we are inwardly aware as we engage in it.

6.) One should notice the difference between " ' "This is a tree" is a judgment' is a judgment" (call this type *J*) and " ' "This is a tree" is true' is true" (which may be called *T*). *J* indicates that mental *acts* are infinite; they can redouble upon themselves without end. *T* indicates the infinity of reflective *objects*.

7.) "Reflection" can be used to designate both the paradigm " 'This is a tree' is a judgment" and also the paradigm " 'This is a tree' is true" because the former includes a reflective element even though it is a reference to a mental act instead of to a physical object. A paradigm for consciousness of a mental act as such would not need to make reference to a foregoing object. "This is a judgment," where "this" refers to a set of words, would be such a nonreflective paradigm. In the terminology adopted here, however, "reflective object" refers to what appears in paradigm (3) above and not in (2).

8.) Daub is undoubtedly castigating Fichte's *Wissenschaftslehre* with its effort to derive all of science from an original "I am."

9.) We should be cautious about reading more out of this development than is warranted, but there is no question that quantum physics
represents a breach with the classical conception of science as found in
Newtonian physics. The typical experiments illustrate the nature of the
change. The two-slit experiment requires an electron gun, a metal
screen with two slits, and a photographic plate on which are recorded
black marks from electrons passing through the slits. A beam of electrons is shot at the screen, and on the photographic plate a pattern of
marks is registered. There are dark bands (that is, bands where the
density of the black marks is high) alternating with light bands (where
the density is low), a frequency pattern or interference pattern like that
of waves when, for example, water passes through two holes in a
breakwater. The interference pattern is caused by the way in which
waves from the two meet. If a crest of one comes together with the crest
of another, they intensify each other; if a crest comes together with a
trough, they cancel each other. This result of the experiment indicates
that electrons have a wavelike character, passing through both slits of
the screen and forming the pattern indicated. The distribution of the
electron marks over the plate is predictable in degrees of probability.

Now one may vary the experiment to see what happens to an individual electron, instead of an ensemble. For this purpose a weak source
is used, so that just one electron leaves a mark on the photographic
plate. But it is continued over a period of time so that a collection of
marks is formed on the plate. Each electron leaves only one mark and
passes through one or the other slit but not through both. This is in
accord with the behavior of a particle instead of a wave. But, surpris-
ingly, as the marks continue to collect on the plate, the pattern formed
is again that of frequency bands, just as it was when a beam of electrons
went through all at once. This reflects not the behavior of particles but
that of waves. Each electron alone goes through just one of the slits, like
a particle and not a wave, but the "performance" of all of them at the
end is like that of a wave and not a particle, since the distribution
pattern is that of waves. What then are these electrons "really" if they
leave a record that attests in part to their being particles and in part to
their being waves?

As a second example, we may consider the single-slit experiment,
which is used to illustrate the Heisenberg uncertainty relations. Suppose that we are interested in predicting the position and velocity of the
electron that passes through a single slit. If the slit is small, then position can be predicted accurately but velocity can be predicted only very

inaccurately. If the slit is large (and the position accordingly uncertain), the velocity can be predicted accurately. In the former case the probability-pattern is spread out at all angles over the whole plate uniformly. In the latter case, the bands are very close together.

These two experiments contravene expectations on two counts. First, electrons behave in part like particles and in part like waves, and it is impossible to picture what kind of entity they must "really" be. In some ways one must view an electron as a wave, in others as a particle. The same is true of the behavior of light. In some cases (such as interference effects) it behaves like a wave; in others (such as photo-electric effects) it behaves like a particle. A unified description of the behavior can be given in a mathematical formalism, but such a unity cannot be pictured. Moreover, the problem is more severe than just the picturability, in a naive realism, of something that has mass (like a billiard ball) but no position (unlike a billiard ball). What is also involved is the problem of measurability at all. This is the second count on which normal expectations are disappointed. For incommensurate variables, such as position and velocity, one must choose to measure the one or the other; it is in principle impossible to do both. For example, in the single-slit measurement, a narrow slit produces a measurement of position but not of velocity, and a wide slit the converse. Both cannot be measured simultaneously. Even more, they cannot be measured sequentially either, because making the first measurement changes the result of the second.

At first it might be thought that the difficulty can be overcome by the same method as used, for example, in measuring the heat capacity of a very small object when the thermometer itself influences the object. One can calculate the heat capacity of the object itself without the disturbance of the thermometer. In a similar way, common-sense seems to tell us, one should be able to calculate the effect a quantum of light has upon an electron which is to be observed through a bombardment with light that disturbs the situation we are trying to study. Yet this is not so. If light quanta of a shorter wave length are used for this purpose, the position of the electron can be located more exactly, yet those quanta have a higher energy and accordingly disturb the electron's velocity all the more. There is no way of calculating what effect the bombardment has upon the electron and hence no way of determining both position and velocity. (The preceding account is based on Ian Barbour, *Issues*, pp. 273-305, and on conversations with William Klink of the Department of Physics and Astronomy at The University of Iowa.)

Chapter II

1.) Tillich modified this position later, though he never repudiated it. See *ST*, I, p. 102; III, pp. 256, 367; and Sidney Hook, ed., *Religious Experience*, pp. 6, 7, 10-11.

2.) The notion of "significant" tautologies is taken from Ian Ramsey, *Religious Language*. Asserting nothing by tautology can become the object of humor, as is shown by a remark in the *New Yorker* magazine of 4 September 1978. The following paragraph was quoted from the Ithaca, N.Y., *Journal*: "The reduction of Japan's trade surplus with the United States hinges on the reduction of Japan's trade surplus with the United States, U.S. Assistant Secretary of Commerce Frank Weil said Monday." Commented the *New Yorker*: "Well said, Assistant Secretary of Commerce Weil!" (p. 96).

3.) In Heidegger's analysis, it is a consequence of the Greek metaphysical heritage when the modern mentality tends to equate the being of an object with how it is placed before us—so that, for example, one thinks the essence of a tree is the way in which it appears to judgment in the unity of a physical perception and a predicative abstraction rather than in the way it opens up possibilities. But if essence lies not necessarily in outward appearance or generic properties but in a possibility opened, then a woodsman's recognition that a tree can be cut down and made into logs for a fireplace to give light and warmth may grasp the essence of the tree more than the judgment "This is a tree." In passing, it might be noted that the ecological movement today seems to stand on a double base: the conservation of this metaphysical attitude, according to which how things naturally appear is closer to their essence than is what may be made of them; and the prophetic warning against the absoluteness of a metaphysical technology, the attitude that things are nothing more or other than what one wills them to be. This mixture of repristination and critique in ecological programs presents dangers of its own.

Chapter 4

1.) That "the true" and "the false" do name objects, even though they are not objects of sensation, is a point that Frege made in his essay "Über Sinn und Bedeutung" (1892). "Every declarative sentence concerned with the reference of its words is . . . to be regarded as a proper name, and its reference, if it has one, is either the True or the False" ("Sense," Geach and Black, p. 63). By a proper name Frege means a sign or combination of signs that "expresses" a sense and "stands for, or designates" a reference (p. 61). In other words, just as the single word "tree" is the name for a physical object, so the whole proposition "This is a tree" is a name for the true (or the false, as the case may be). The proposition designates and stands for the true, as the word stands for the object tree.

2.) Ricoeur uses the phrase "being like" to designate a certain unity of being and nonbeing in "metaphorical" statements, such as those in parables: "The kingdom of heaven *is like* a man who went out, etc." This is not simile or metaphor in the normal sense because, unlike the subject in such expressions as "The man is a lion," the subject "the kingdom of heaven" is the unknown, that which is yet to be shown in the course of the parable. Hence the sense of the parabolic introduction "The kingdom of heaven is like" is really this: "The kingdom of heaven *is* the kingdom of heaven *as*" what is then told in the parable. A parable does not tell us what the kingdom of heaven is like, but where to look in order to see *as* what the kingdom of heaven *is* what it is. For this reason the phrase "being like" is less exact an account of the being involved here than is "being . . . as."

Bibliography

The works listed below are either quoted or mentioned in the book, with the exception of those marked with an asterisk; these are works used but not cited by name. Short titles used for reference are given in brackets behind each entry.

Altizer, Thomas J. J. *The Self-Embodiment of God.* New York: Harper & Row, 1977. [*Self-Embodiment*]

Anselm. *"Proslogium," "Monologium," "An Appendix in Behalf of the Fool" by Gaunilon, and "Cur Deus Homo."* Translated by Sidney Norton Deane. La Salle, Il.: The Open Court Publishing Co., 1951. [*Prosl.*]

Arendt, Hannah. *The Life of the Mind*, 2 vols. New York: Harcourt Brace Jovanovich, 1977-78. [*Life*]

Aristotle. *The Metaphysics.* With an English translation by Hugh Tredennick. Loeb Classical Library 271. Cambridge, Ma.: Harvard University Press, 1968 (1933). [*Met.*]

————. *Posterior Analytics, Topica.* Loeb Classical Library 391. Cambridge, Ma.: Harvard University Press, 1966 (1960). [*Post.An., Topics*]

Augustine. *Confessiones.* Munich: Kösel-Verlag, 1955. [*Conf.*]

————. *Principia Dialecticae.* In *Patrologiae Cursus Completus*, edited by J. P. Migne, vol. 32, pp. 1409-1420. Paris: Garnier Fratres, 1877. [*Princ. Dial.*]

Ayer, Alfred Jules. *Language, Truth and Logic.* New York: Dover Publications, 1946. [*Language*]

Barbour, Ian G. *Issues in Science and Religion.* Englewood Cliffs, N.J.: Prentice-Hall, Inc., 1966. [*Issues*]

Barth, H. M. " 'Fides creatrix divinitatis.' " *Neue Zeitschrift für systematische Theologie und Religionsphilosophie* 14,1 (1972), 89-106. ["Fides"]

Barth, Karl. *Fides quaerens intellectum: Anselms Beweis der Existenz Gottes im Zusammenhang seines theologischen Programms.* 2nd ed. Zollikon: Evangelischer Verlag, 1958. [*F*]

————. *Kirchliche Dogmatik.* Vols. I/1 and II/1. Zollikon: Evangelischer Verlag, 1957, 1958. [*KD*]

————. *Der Römerbrief.* Unaltered reprint of the first edition of 1919. Zürich: EVZ-Verlag, 1963. [*Rb(1)*]

————. "Das Wort Gottes als Aufgabe der Theologie." In *Anfänge der dialektischen Theologie*, edited by Jürgen Moltmann, vol. I, pp. 197-218. Munich: Kaiser Verlag, 1966. ["Wort"]

Bartley, William Warren III. *Wittgenstein.* Philadelphia: J. P. Lippincott Co., 1973. [*Wittgenstein*]

Bonaventure. *Itinerarium mentis in Deum* and *De reductione artium ad theologiam.* Munich: Kösel-Verlag, 1961. [*Itinerarium*]

Cassien, Jean. *Conférences.* Vol. II. Latin text with French translation by Dom E. Pichery. Paris: Les Éditions du Cerf, 1958. [*Conf.*]

*Christian, William A. *Meaning and Truth in Religion.* Princeton, N.J.: Princeton University Press, 1964. [*Meaning and Truth*]

Cummings, E. E. "Jottings." in *i: six nonlectures.* Cambridge, Ma.: Harvard University Press, 1972 (c1953). ["Jottings"]

Daub, Carl. "Über den Logos. Ein Beitrag zur Logik der göttlichen Namen." *Theologische Studien und Kritiken* 6 (1833), 355-410. ["Logos"]

————. *Philosophische und theologische Vorlesungen.* Vol. VI. Edited by Marheineke and Dittenberger. Berlin: Verlag von Duncker und Humblot, 1841. [*Vorl.*, VI]

Des Pres, Terrence. "Goodness Incarnate." Review of Philip Hallie, *Lest Innocent Blood Be Shed. Harper's* 258, 1548 (May 1979), 83-86. ["Goodness"]

Ebeling, Gerhard. *Dogmatik des christlichen Glaubens.* Vol. I. Tübingen: J. C. B. Mohr (Paul Siebeck), 1979. [*Dogmatik*]

————. "Existenz zwischen Gott und Gott." *Zeitschrift für Theologie und Kirche* 62,1 (May 1965), 86-111. ["Existenz"]

————. *God and Word.* Translated by James W. Leitch. Philadelphia: Fortress Press, 1967. [*G&W*]

Feuerbach, Ludwig. *The Essence of Christianity.* Translated by George Eliot. New York: Harper & Row, Torchbook edition, 1957. [*Essence*]

————. *Das Wesen des Glaubens im Sinne Luthers.* In *Sämtliche Werke*, Vol. VII, pp. 311-375. Stuttgart: Fromann Verlag Günther Holzboog, 1960. [*Wesen des Glaubens*]

————. *Des Wesen der Religion.* Leipzig: Alfred Kröner, 1851. [*WR*]

Fichte, Johann. *Grundlage der gesamten Wissenschaftslehre als Handschrift für seine Zuhörer* (1974). Hamburg: Felix Meiner Verlag, 1970. [*Wissenschaftslehre*]

Frege, Gottlob. "On Sense and Reference." In *Translations from the*

Philosophical Writings of Gottlob Frege, edited by P. T. Geach and Max Black, pp. 56-78. 2nd ed. Oxford: Basil Blackwell, 1960. ["Sense"]

Gadamer, Hans-Georg. *Truth and Method*. Translated from the 2nd German edition. New York: Seabury Press, 1975. [*TM*]

―――. *Wahrheit und Methode*. 2nd edition, expanded by a *Nachtrag*. Tübingen: J. C. B. Mohr (Paul Siebeck), 1965. [*WuM*]

Hallie, Philip. *Lest Innocent Blood Be Shed: The Story of the Village of Le Chambon and How Goodness Happened There*. New York: Harper & Row, 1979. [*Lest*]

Hare, R. M. "Theology and Falsification: The *University* Discussion." In *New Essays in Philosophical Theology*, edited by Anthony Flew and Alisdair MacIntyre, pp. 99-103. London: SCM Press, 1955. ["Theol."]

Hartshorne, Charles. *Anselm's Discovery: A Re-examination of the Ontological Proof for God's Existence*. La Salle, Il.: The Open Court Publishing Company, 1965. [*AD*]

Hegel, G. W. F. "Glauben und Wissen." In *Werke in zwanzig Bänden*, vol. 2: *Jenaer Schriften 1801-1807*. Frankfurt am Main: Suhrkamp Verlag, 1970. ["Glauben und Wissen"]

―――. *Wissenschaft der Logik*. In *Werke in zwanzig Bänden*, Vols. 5 & 6. Frankfurt am Main: Suhrkamp Verlag, 1969. [*WdL*]

Heidegger, Martin. "The ˙ Onto-theo-logical Constitution of Metaphysics." In *Identity and Difference*. English and German text. Translation with Introduction by Joan Stambaugh. New York: Harper & Row, 1969. ["Onto-theo-logical"]

―――. *Sein und Zeit*. Tübingen: Max Niemeyer Verlag, 1963. [*SuZ*]

―――. *Vom Wesen der Wahrheit*. Frankfurt am Main: Klostermann, 1949. [*Wesen*]

Heisenberg, Werner. "Kausalgesetz und Quantenmechanik." *Erkenntnis*, vol. II (1931), and *Annalen der Philosophie*, X, 172-182. ["Kausalgesetz"]

Herrmann, Wilhelm. *The Communion of the Christian with God*. Translated by J. S. Sandys Stanyon, revised by R. W. Stewart. London: Williams & Norgate Ltd., 1970. [*Communion*]

Hochstaffl, Josef. *Negative Theologie: Ein Versuch zur Vermittlung des patristischen Begriffs*. Munich: Kösel-Verlag, 1976. [*Neg. Theol.*]

Hodgson, Peter. "Heidegger, Revelation, and the Word of God." *Journal of Religion* 49,3 (1969), 228-252. ["Heidegger"]

Holmer, Paul. *The Grammar of Faith*. New York: Harper & Row, 1978. [*Grammar*]

Hook, Sidney, ed. *Religious Experience and Truth*. New York: New York University Press, 1961. [*Rel. Exp.*]

Ignatius. *To the Magnesians*. In *The Apostolic Fathers*, vol. 1, with English translation by Kirsopp Lake. Loeb Classical Library. Cambridge, Ma.: Harvard University Press, 1949. [*Mag.*]

Jäger, Alfred. *Gott: Nochmals Martin Heidegger.* Tübingen: J. C. B. Mohr (Paul Siebeck), 1978. [*Gott*]

James, William. *The Meaning of Truth.* New York: Longmans, Green & Co., 1910. [*Meaning*]

Jenson, Robert. *God After God: The God of the Past and the God of the Future Seen in the Work of Karl Barth.* Indianapolis: The Bobbs-Merrill Co., 1969. [*God*]

Kant, Immanuel. *Critique of Pure Reason.* Translated by Norman Kemp Smith. London: Macmillan & Company Ltd., 1958. [*CrPuR*]

*Kerényi, Karl. "Theos: 'Gott'—auf Griechisch" (1968). In *Antike Religion*, pp. 207-217. Darmstadt: Wissenschaftliche Buchgesellschaft, 1971. ["Theos"]

Kierkegaard, Sören. *Fear and Trembling.* Garden City, N.Y.: Doubleday Anchor Books, 1954 (© 1941 by Princeton University Press). [*FT*]

Kretzmann, Norman. "Semantics: History of." In *The Encyclopedia of Philosophy* 7, pp. 358-406. New York: The Macmillan Company and The Free Press, 1967. ["Semantics"]

Luther, Martin. *Werke: Kritische Gesamtausgabe.* Weimar: H. Böhlau, 1883- . [*WA*]

Pannenberg, Wolfhart. *Jesus—God and Man.* Translated by Lewis L. Wilkins and Duane A. Priebe. Philadelphia: The Westminster Press, 1968. [*Jesus*]

Pascal, Blaise. *Pensées.* With an English translation by H. F. Stewart. New York: Pantheon Books, 1950. [*Pensées*]

Picht, Georg. "Die Epiphanie der ewigen Gegenwart: Wahrheit, Sein und Erscheinung bei Parmenides." In *WVV* pp. 36-86. ["Epiphanie"]

————. "Der Gott der Philosophen." In *WVV*, pp. 229-251. ["Gott"]

————. *Wahrheit, Vernunft, Verantwortung: Philosophische Studien.* Stuttgart: Ernst Klett Verlag, 1969. [*WVV*]

———— and Rudolf, Enno. *Theologie—Was ist das?* Stuttgart: Kreuz-Verlag, 1977. [*Theologie*]

Pitcher, George, ed. *Truth.* Englewood Cliffs, N.J.: Prentice-Hall, 1964. [*Truth*]

Pivčević, Edo. "Truth as Structure." *Review of Metaphysics* 28,2 (1974), 311-327. ["Truth"]

Plato. *Cratylus.* With English translation by H. N. Fowler. Loeb Classical Library. Cambridge, Ma.: Harvard University Press, 1970. [*Cratylus*]

Rahner, Karl. "Anonymous Christians" (1964). In *Theological Investigations*, vol. VI, pp. 390-398. Baltimore: Helicon Press, 1969. ["Anonymous"]

————. *Geist in Welt. Zur Metaphysik der endlichen Erkenntnis bei Thomas von Aquin.* Unaltered reprint of the 2nd edition of 1957. Munich: Kösel-Verlag, 1964. [*Geist*]

Ramsey, F. P. "Facts and Propositions." In *Truth*, edited by Pitcher. ["Facts"]

Ramsey, Ian T. *Religious Language: An Empirical Placing of Theological Phrases.* New York: The Macmillan Company, 1963. (© 1957). [*Religious Language*]

————. *Words About God: The Philosophy of Religion.* London: SCM Press Ltd., 1971. [*Words*]

Ricoeur, Paul. "Existence and Hermeneutics." In *The Philosophy of Paul Ricoeur*, edited by Charles E. Reagan and David Stewart, pp. 97-108. Boston: Beacon Press, 1978. ["Existence and Hermeneutics"]

————. *Fallible Man.* Translated by Charles Kelbley. Chicago: Henry Regnery Company, Gateway Editions, n.d. [*FM*]

Rubenstein, Richard. *After Auschwitz.* Indianapolis: The Bobbs-Merrill Co., 1966. [*Auschwitz*]

Ryle, Gilbert. "Systematically Misleading Expressions" (1952) and *The Concept of Mind* (1949). Selections in *Words*, edited by Ramsey, pp. 128-138.

Schleiermacher, Friedrich. *The Christian Faith.* Translated by H. R. Mackintosh and J. S. Stewart. Edinburgh: T. & T. Clark, 1928. [*CF*]

Schütz, Ludwig. *Thomas-Lexikon.* 2nd, greatly enlarged edition. Paderborn: Druck und Verlag von Ferdinand Schöningh, 1895. [*Thomas-Lexikon*]

Schweizer, Carl G. "Geist bei Hegel und Heiliger Geist." *Neue Zeitschrift für systematische Theologie und Religionsphilosophie* 6 (1964), 318-328. ["Geist"]

Sherry, Patrick. *Religion, Truth and Language Games.* New York: Barnes & Noble, 1977.

*Simon, Ulrich. *A Theology of Auschwitz: The Christian Faith and the Problem of Evil.* Atlanta: John Knox Press, 1979 (© 1967). [*Theology*]

Strawson, Peter F. "A Problem About Truth–A Reply to Mr. Warnock." In *Truth*, edited by Pitcher. ["Problem"]

Tertullian. *De carne Christi.* In *Patrologiae Cursus Completus*, vol. 2, edited by J. P. Migne. Paris: Garnier Fratres, 1879. [*De carne Christi*]

Theunissen, Michael. "Begriff und Realität. Hegels Aufhebung des metaphysischen Wahrheitsbegriffs." In *Denken im Schatten des Nihilismus: Festschrift für Wilhelm Weischedel zum 70. Geburstag*, edited by Alexander Schwan. Darmstadt: Wissenschaftliche Buchgesellschaft, 1975. ["Begriff"]

Thomas Aquinas. *On the Truth of the Catholic Faith: Summa contra Gen-*

tiles. Translation with Introduction and Notes by Anton C. Pegis. New York: Doubleday Image, 1955. [*CG*]

————. *Summa theologiae.* 3 vols. Turin and Rome: Marietti, 1952-56. [*S.th.*]

Tillich, Paul. *Biblical Religion and the Search for Ultimate Reality.* Chicago: University of Chicago Press, 1955. [*BR*]

————. *Dynamics of Faith.* New York: Harper & Row, 1957. [*DF*]

————. *Mysticism and Guilt-Consciousness in Schelling's Philosophical Development.* Translated with Introduction by Victor Nuovo. Lewisburg, Pa.; Bucknell University Press, 1974. [*Mysticism*]

————. "Philosophie und Religion." In *Gesammelte Werke*, vol. V, pp. 101-108. Stuttgart: Evangelisches Verlagswerk, 1964. Reprint of "Philosophie: III. Philosophie und Religion, grundsätzlich," *Religion in Geschichte und Gegenwart*, 2nd edition (1930). ["Phil.u.Rel."]

————. "Religionsphilosophie" (1925). In *Gesammelte Werke*, vol. I: *Frühe Hauptwerke*, pp. 297-364. Stuttgart: Evangelisches Verlagswerk, 1959. ["Religionsphilosophie"]

————. *Systematic Theology.* 3 vols. Chicago: University of Chicago Press, 1951-1963. [*ST*]

————. Theses on Christology, 1911. *Vorträge Kassel.* Typescript. Göttingen: Paul-Tillich-Archiv. [Theses on Christology]

Ueltzen, Hans Dieter. " 'Gott selbst ist tot': Historische Bemerkungen zur Entstehung des Liedes und der Rede vom Tode Gottes." *Evangelische Theologie* 36,6 (1976), 563-567. [" 'Gott' "]

Vogel, Heinrich. "Wann ist ein theologischer Satz wahr?" *Kerygma und Dogma* 4 (1958), 176-190. ["Wahr"]

*Wagner, Hans. *Philosophie und Reflexion.* Munich: Ernst Reinhardt Verlag, 1959. [*Phil.*]

White, Alan R. *Truth.* Garden City, N.Y.: Doubleday Anchor, 1970. [*Truth*]

Wittgenstein, Ludwig. *Philosophische Bemerkungen.* Edited by Rush Rhees. Oxford: Basil Blackwell, 1964. [*Phil. Bemerk.*]

Index

197

cal, 113, 114, 118, 123, 128; third, 176

Logic, 86, 140, 184 n.2

Luther, Martin, 40–41, 42, 43, 44, 105

M

Manifestation, 137

Meaning, 4, 89–90, 135, 154; and reality, 23, 30, 158, 174; as life of mind, 3; as referent, 135; distinct from reflective object, 3; of words and of things, 53, 81, 82–83, 92–93, 166; of being a subject, 128; question of, 138; religious, 50. *See also* Sense

Memory, 14

Messiah, 37–38

Metalanguage, 176

Metanoein (afterthinking), 155

Metaphysics, 5–6, 14–15, 50, 51, 60, 158, 188 n.3

Method, 40

Moonlanding (1969), 117

N

Narrative, 123–24

"Natural man," 41

Nature, 43–44

Negation, 90–93; double, 60; God as, 176

Negator, 141–42

Nietzsche, Friedrich, 10, 15, 44

Nihilism, 10, 44

Nirvana, 182

Noema (*noesis*), 127

Nothing, 84, 131, 151, 168, 188 n.2

Notion, 80, 85. *See also* Concept; Percept; Understanding

O

Object: and kerygma, 102; as word, 174; God as negation of, 171–72; in itself, 101; kinds of, 2, 3, 6, 25–26, 27, 153, 154

Objectivity, 40

One, 15, 66, 68, 70–71

Omnipotence, 37, 140, 165

Ontology, 15

Openness, 151, 153, 171, 184 n.2

Otherness, 136, 155, 176

P

Panentheism, 87

Pannenberg, Wolfhart, 106–9

Parable: truth of, 52–55

Paradigm, 25–27, 154, 185 n.4

Paradox, 37

Parmenides, 60

Particles, elementary, 46

Pascal, Blaise, 94

Percept (perception), 24, 47–48, 80

Performance, 25

Person, announcing, 99–100

Personhood, 73

Perspective, 32

Phenomenology, 30, 87; reduction in, 127–29

Philosophy: and religion, 96; God in, 16; of religion, 27, 61

Physics, 44–46, 133

Picht, Georg, 15, 16, 124

Pivčević, Edo, 17

Plato, 15, 25

Play, 72–74. *See also* Game; Tennis; Truth

Pluralism, 40

Point of view, 31, 128

Poitivism, 17

Prayer, 109–10

Predicate: as property or action, 65; as showing or defining, 78–79; creation of new, 36; two kinds of, 71

Prethought, 154, 157

Prime mover, 75–76